A GUIDE FOR CO-OPS, INTERNS AND FULL-TIME JOB SEEKERS

FIND YOUR
FIRST
PROFESSIONAL JOB

Scott Weighart

This textbook is dedicated to Tim Hall and Jan Wohlberg, the two mentors who were the most helpful and influential in beginning my career in academia.

CONTENTS

ACKNOWLEDGEMENTS

Given that this book has been a work-in-progress since 1995, many people have played important roles in the ongoing development of this book. My business co-op colleague Donna Smith helped me get started with material on resume writing. My co-op colleagues Mel Simms and Betsey Blackmer shared their co-op preparation materials early on, giving me useful perspectives on how to write this book.

The business co-op faculty has provided feedback on the text over the last six years; this has been a tremendous help in revising and improving the book dramatically with each of our internal editions. In particular, Charlie Bognanni, Bill Sloane, and Elizabeth Chilvers have seen this book through from its earliest days and have always been supportive. I am fortunate to work with a terrific group in business co-op. Our management group (Linda O'Connor, Bill Munze, and Katie Meller) inspired the new Appendix A with their materials on co-op logistics, a section also influenced by works of our Arts and Sciences co-op counterpart Melissa McDaniels.

The biggest improvement reflected in this edition is definitely the sidebar boxes that offer the perspectives of some very experienced co-op faculty at Northeastern University. Thanks to Rose Dimarco, Ronnie Porter, and Bob Tillman for contributing their perspectives: This broadened the reach of this new edition significantly. Likewise, I am very grateful to Marie Sacino of LaGuardia Community College for giving us perspectives regarding students and employers from her institution. I am so impressed with the energy and ideas coming out of LaGuardia. Many of our Northeastern University students and employers deserve thanks. In particular, thanks to our MGT1002 Big Siblings (Ted Schneider, Mark Moccia, and Keith Laughman) for expansively and passionately including their ideas here. My MIS alum Gabriel Glasscock also contributed their thoughts, adding valuable additional perspectives. As for co-op employers, Myretta Robens of Harvard Business School Publishing, Steve Sim of Microsoft, and Mike Naclerio of the workplace HELPline were kind enough to offer their thoughts for publication.

Thanks also to those who have brought this book a long way in terms of its appearance. Victoria Arico greatly enhanced the professionalism of the book with her cover design. Marjorie Apel from Manhattan College gave me valuable feedback on the book's style, and Alison Molumby gave us great ideas for redesigning the text for this edition. Lastly, my wife Ellie came through as desktop publisher and proofreader *extraordinaire* on this edition, and as a result we have our best-looking book to date! Thanks to everyone.

Scott Weighart
August 2003

INTRODUCTION

Being successful in your first professional job is not magic: It requires a positive attitude and the willingness to keep taking small steps toward self-improvement in your career. Whether you are planning for you first co-op job, internship, or first full-time job out of college, this guidebook was written to show you exactly what separates the extraordinary new professional from those who are ordinary or mediocre. Follow these steps carefully, and you can transform yourself into a great job candidate and performer.... a little at a time.

Find Your First Professional Job was initially written to be a key resource for business students at Northeastern University, which has one of the largest co-op programs in the world. Yet although a Northeastern-specific version of this guidebook has been used with thousands of students, this edition is geared to offering much of the same reliable and time-tested information to students in other programs. Although Northeastern's students use this information as a resource on everything from sprucing up their resume to dealing with multiple job offers in our business co-op program, I have broadened the aim of this guidebook to provide more useful support to co-ops, interns, and full-time job seekers in all majors and at colleges and universities anywhere.

At this point in time, universities across the country are embracing multiple forms of practice-oriented education, including co-op, internships, practicum assignments, volunteer work/community service learning, work abroad, and clinical rotations to name a few. Basically, the rising cost of higher education has resulted in students and parents asking, "What return will I get on my investment in higher education?" As a direct result, schools ranging from small community colleges to big-name Ivy League institutions have found it necessary to give their students more opportunities to get real-world experience.

This is a terrific development for the 21st-century student: Working in your field gives you a chance to test out a career, build a resume and reference, make meaningful connections between the classroom and the real world, create connections with post-graduation employers, and—often but not always—earn money.

While this represents a great opportunity, it also creates challenges for students. Some of these challenges relate to planning your co-op or internship: Will professional organizations want to hire you when your job experience is limited to retail, restaurant work, and childcare? What can you do right now to increase your chances of getting the best possible job—even if you don't intend to look for your first job for a year or more? How will the job market affect your search? What are your job search options? The first chapter of this guidebook, "Planning Ahead For Your First Professional Job" tackles these questions.

Other challenges arise during the preparation stage—the weeks and months immediately preceding your co-op job, internship, or other work-related endeavor. How can you write an effective resume when your best job was working as a Burger King cashier or as a babysitter for families in your neighborhood? What should you include and emphasize on your resume, and what is best to leave off? How can you overcome your jitters about interviewing and present yourself positively but honestly? How can you deal with fuzzy open-ended questions, tough interviewers, and the fact that you can't possibly anticipate all questions that may be asked. What do you if you get an offer from Company A when you're waiting for Company B to get back to you? Chapter 2 ("Writing An Effective Resume") and Chapter 3 ("Strategic Interviewing") of the guidebook cover this terrain and much more.

Once you have lined up your work experience, the real work begins. What is at stake when you are working as a co-op? How can you live up to your interview and make the most of your co-op opportunity? How can you balance a part-time internship with full-time classes? What should you do if problems arise? How can you get the best possible evaluation and reference? Chapter 4 reviews "Keys To On-The-Job Success" in handling these concerns among others.

You also may wonder about how to make sense out what happened during your co-op or internship when you return to campus for classes. What steps might be required of you when you return to school? What might you need to do to get credit for your work experience? What are some options to consider as you process the experience? Chapter 5 goes over "Making Sense Of Your First Professional Experience" and considers the reflection steps that are required at NU and many other institutions.

Lastly, there are two brand-new appendices in this edition of the guidebook. Appendix A details job search logistics and NU's Co-op Learning Model. This is a great chapter for understanding the job search process as well as the steps involved in learning from practical experience. Appendix B covers how to write effective cover letters, whether you are looking for a co-op job or pursuing your first full-time job after graduation. This is a long overdue inclusion, and it should prove useful to all students, sooner or later.

This book has been through numerous editions and has been used by thousands of Northeastern University students and hundreds of students at LaGuardia Community College in New York. As such, the material here is tested by experience—just as you will be as you go through your first professional job experiences. While this is certainly serious business, I have tried to write the book in a light and conversational way, including many real-life anecdotes and quotes to make the book as fun to read as it is informative. It's really exciting for me to have the voices of some of our best co-op students included in the guidebook. You'll find these thoughtful perspectives in sidebar boxes.

Here's an example.

For the first time, this guidebook now includes the perspectives of other co-op faculty from outside the College of Business Administration and even from outside Northeastern University. At NU, I interviewed three of our most experienced co-op faculty—Bob Tillman in the College of Engineering; Ronnie Porter in the College of Arts and Sciences, and Rose Dimarco from the Bouvé College of Health Sciences. I also have been fortunate to add the perspectives of Marie Sacino at LaGuardia Community College in the form of sidebar boxes and new sample resumes from outside my university. All of these viewpoints are a tremendous addition to the book, as they give students a sense of how different— and similar—it can be if you are seeking your first professional job as an arts and sciences student or aspiring health-care professional or engineer. You might be surprised at how much a student in ANY major can learn by reading and reflecting on advice from these various perspectives.

Like most aspects of being a first-time professional in the workplace, what you get out of this guidebook will depend heavily on the amount of effort you spend in truly understanding the material that we present to you here. If you just skim through the chapters, you will find that this text is no more useful than giving a menu to a starving man.

If, however, you really put some energy into thinking about how this material applies to you and incorporating these concepts into how you approach resume-writing, interviewing, and your actual co-op job, you will find that these principles will help you in your career long after you have graduated.

I hope that this book helps you gain confidence as you approach your first co-op job, internship, clinical experience, practicum, or full-time job after graduation. Good luck in your preparation activities and in all of your efforts to professionalize yourself in the weeks and months to come. You might just amaze yourself with the results!

Scott Weighart
August 2003

CHAPTER ONE
Planning For Your First Professional Job

Whether you work in a co-op job or internship, a clinical assignment or simply your first full-time job after graduation, you have a great deal at stake. Yet even though many students now realize how important some form of practical job experience is these days, not all students really understand everything that they're going to get out of the experience. Additionally, many students fail to realize that there is a great deal that can be done to get ready for a co-op or internship—even if their first professional job is months and months away.

This chapter is intended to get you thinking about your next professional job *now* so you will have a better understanding of the benefits of getting practical job experience and what you can do to give yourself a head start on the process.

BENEFITS OF PROFESSIONAL EXPERIENCE

For all undergraduates getting real-world experience, there are still many common themes when we consider the benefits of doing a co-op job, internship, clinical assignment, or practicum before graduation.

Career Testing: In any form of what we at Northeastern University call "practice-oriented education," getting practical work experience as an undergrad helps you test out different careers. This will help you determine whether you are on the right career path. It's one thing to be in a finance class for three or four hours per week: It's a whole different ballgame working in a finance job 40 hours per week for a summer or six months. You really wouldn't want to spend $50,000 to 100,000 or more on your education over four years, only to find out six months into your first "real job" that you actually *dislike* working in that field as a full-time professional. What do you do then? Go back to school?

It's not at all uncommon to see the following scenario with our students at Northeastern University: John Schlabotnik goes to see his co-op coordinator right after completing his first co-op job experience in human services (or accounting or physical therapy or any other major). The co-op coordinator welcomes John back and asks how the job went. "What did you *learn* on your job, John?" John blushes, looks at the ground, and sheepishly says, "Uhhh, I think I learned that I don't want to *be* in human services."

It's almost as if John thinks that his co-op coordinator will criticize or condemn him for such rebellious thinking! Hardly. We remind the student that this is a primary purpose of internships and co-op, and then we can begin a dialogue about what other concentration or major may be more appropriate.

Career Testing – An Engineering Co-op Perspective
by Bob Tillman
Most of the students I have coming in want fieldwork. And then when they do it, they don't want it anymore. Okay, well, tell me what that means: What changed? How hard was it? What does it feel like when people scream and yell at you? You know, you're only as good as your last mistake—and that's big in engineering, especially civil. And when you're the engineer or the super some day, how are you going to handle it differently? Remember what it felt like to be a beginner.

Bob Tillman is a cooperative education faculty coordinator
in Civil Engineering at Northeastern University.

I have known more than a few physical therapy students at Northeastern who absolutely loved the subject in the classroom. During their first field experience, however, a few found out that they felt amazingly uncomfortable having to touch people in their role as a physical therapist in training. For most, this was a startling and upsetting realization—but also an absolutely critical discovery that led them to make a necessary change very early in their college careers.

See another example in the sidebar box on the next page.

Experience Building
You may not begin your first internship or co-op with much directly relevant job experience on your resume, but you can change that fact dramatically over the course of a few real-world experiences. How this happens will vary depending on a few different factors.

If you begin your undergraduate years with a very clear sense of your career goals—and if your real-world experience merely confirms those goals for you—you will graduate with great *depth* of experience. For example, I primarily work with Management Information Systems students at Northeastern University. Student A may know before she even meets with me that she wants to be a

Network Administrator. Even if she has no direct experience, we can ensure that she ends up with in-depth knowledge of the field after completing three six-

---

Confirming Career Plans At LaGuardia Community College
by Marie Sacino

An internship can provide an opportunity to discover your passion, to make a solid contribution to your employer, and to grow. Zoe Cornielle, a liberal arts student in our social science and humanities curriculum, explored her interest in the field of social work during her first internship at the Hospital for Special Surgery. Zoe was assigned to work in the Department of Patient Care and Quality Management. Under the supervision of a program coordinator and a managed care associate, Zoe worked as part of a health care team to provide education, advocacy, and assistance to outpatients in both rheumatology and orthopedic clinics.

With training, support and supervision from social work professionals, Zoe began to provide outreach services to patients in various patient waiting areas. Zoe listened to patients' concerns and questions, provided information on education and support groups, made referrals to community based agencies, and kept records of patient activity.

On my visit to HSS, I got a first-hand opportunity to see Zoe at work. I was so impressed by her professionalism, her ability to engage patients, her understanding and sensitivity of the impact of barriers to health care as well as her dedication to the patients with whom she worked. HSS was also quite impressed: Zoe was invited back for her second full-time internship this past summer. She discovered her passion—helping people—and confirmed her career plans: social work. Zoe expanded her role greatly as she took on the new role of "first" lead volunteer. She had an opportunity to participate in developing training materials and in leading group discussions. Zoe also provided support and supervision to new interns and trainees as they began to work with patients. She now plans to transfer to Hunter College to pursue a degree in social work.

Marie Sacino is an Associate Professor of Cooperative Education at LaGuardia Community College.

---

month co-op jobs. Maybe her first job is a rather light Help Desk job. With that on her resume, she is able to get a substantial PC/LAN position next time around, complete with opportunities to troubleshoot problems, upgrade software on the network, and perform fundamentals of networking such as adding new users. On her third co-op, she might be doing substantial computer room work, handling tricky interface issues between Novell NetWare and TCP/IP, maybe even setting up the hubs and routers that form the "guts" of the network. She graduates with a rich and deep understanding of one part of MIS.

Meanwhile, Student B doesn't really know what he wants to do with MIS—he just knows that he likes doing stuff with computers. Maybe he starts out with that same Help Desk job but finds it frustrating to deal with impatient end users and to juggle competing priorities and requests amidst numerous interruptions. Next time around, he tries a database development position and likes it more but finds it too much on the opposite extreme—too much time sitting at his computer, not enough variety. Finally, he gets a Systems Analyst job on his third co-op and acts as a go-between for programmers and financial planners who need software. This student graduates with greater *breadth* of experience. He may not command as much money in his first full-time job, but he may have more options available to him now and more doors open to him later. So there are positives either way.

Additionally, any professional experience that you obtain as an undergrad will do more than improve your technical skills in a given field—the experience will provide you with great opportunities to professionalize yourself. While most students come into internships and co-ops focusing on what technical skills they may be able to acquire, many come away from their first job rather surprised at how much they learn about working that has *nothing to do with learning technical skills and responsibilities*. Every workplace has its own written and unwritten rules about performance and behavior. Organizational politics can have a dramatic impact on your ability to function effectively in a position. Supervisors can vary dramatically in terms of their managerial skills, expectations, and pet peeves. Developing the adaptability to handle different work environments and to obtain great evaluations in situations that require radically different behavior can be a big challenge. Learning the changing rules of the game and making sure that you succeed regardless of varying expectations is a characteristic of the best future professionals.

Most students—especially those working full-time hours in their work experience—find that they feel more confident about their professionalism after each job experience. The discipline required to get to work on time every day and to get your work done well and on time seems to develop good habits that become more automatic over time in most cases. It's often exciting for a co-op or internship coordinator to see a student after one job experience: I often am amazed to see big changes in professional etiquette when these students return to my office and interact with me. Frequently, going to work in a professional setting helps you develop a greater sense of purpose both in the classroom and in your professional relationships.

Building a great resume and getting valuable references
If you're building your experience, then you obviously are also building an impressive resume detailing all of that experience. Just as importantly, if you perform well, you can end up with a long list of respected professionals who will recommend you to future employers. Developing a network of people who are able and willing to assist your future job searches can make a big difference— many jobs are filled through personal connections rather than simply pulling in a bunch of anonymous candidates through newspaper ads.

Enjoying a trial period with potential full-time employers

Many organizations who hire students for co-op jobs, internships, and other forms of practice-oriented learning are looking for more than a person to do a job for six months—they are using the co-op period to "test out" someone that they may or may not wish to make a job offer to upon graduation.

As one large co-op employer told me: "If we hire ten co-op students, we figure that at least nine of them will work out well and get productive work done in a cost-effective manner. If three of those nine are such stars that we want to hire them after graduation, then that's really the ultimate goal for us. After all, at our company, we can't just fire someone—we have to coach them to death!"

Indeed, this organization doesn't allow managers to fire employees who are clearly poor performers. Instead, the manager must hold regular "coaching meetings" and document them heavily. In the end, the employee still ends up being terminated. As you might imagine, this employer really doesn't want to hire the wrong people—that's a mistake that costs thousands of dollars in addition to causing numerous headaches! Hiring co-ops helps them know what they're getting and makes it less likely that they will have to go down that costly and time-consuming path with a wayward employee.

Integrating classroom learning with workplace learning

Certainly one of the greatest payoffs for students who immerse themselves in a relevant real-world setting is the opportunity to make meaningful connections between theory and practice. Better still, it's a two-way street: Concepts that are hard to really understand in the classroom can come alive for you when you see how they apply to real-world situations. At other times, you will learn how to do something while on co-op but perhaps not really understand the underlying concepts until you learn about them in a class after completing your work experience.

Better still, co-op, clinicals, and internships can bring home the importance of classroom concepts, sometimes in dramatic and unexpected ways. Students who don't get meaningful, career-related job experiences during their undergraduate years sometimes have a harder time believing that some required courses are all that important. Even if you have a gifted professor, it may be hard for a student to believe that coursework in finance or accounting has any relevance to them if they "know" that their future is in MIS or Human Resources.

Getting that professional experience as an undergrad can reveal that this way of thinking is an illusion. One of my students who just completed an MIS position in senior management support at The Gillette Company had to provide computer and audiovisual assistance to some of the most powerful people in the organization. His coursework in accounting took on a newfound urgency for him as he ended up assisting during several heavy number-crunching meetings, in which the executives spoke with great passion about balance sheets, income statements, and other concepts that the student had found only mildly interesting before the job began.

Another student felt rather lukewarm about taking his Organizational Behavior requirement, mainly because our NU offering is an eight-credit course meeting twice a week for over three hours at a time. Before long, he found that his class with Professor Brendan Bannister was "almost like therapy." It helped him process and understand many elements of motivation, leadership, and group dynamics that had absolutely baffled and confounded him on his previous co-op job.

Coursework outside of your major also can have a dramatic impact on your career, and vice-versa. One of the biggest mistakes students make when picking electives is to just pick something that sounds relatively painless without considering the possible benefits of liberal arts electives. A marketing student might be well-advised to take a communications course that helps build public speaking skills; a civil engineering student with lofty aspirations might be wise to take classes in corporate finance. I knew a student who felt that her self-confidence and interpersonal skills improved dramatically by taking a class in acting. Likewise, there can be good synergy for computer science students and modern languages majors who take some electives in each other's disciplines.

One of the funniest stories along these lines came from one of my students who absolutely had to add a social science course to meet a liberal arts requirement for business students. He signed up for Introduction to Psychological Counseling, basically because the class hadn't filled up yet and it fit the requirement. When his next co-op ended up being a PC support job, he couldn't believe his dumb luck: He was shocked to find himself using techniques he had learned in class—such as active listening—when trying to calm down and help computer users who were frequently angry, embittered, and impatient due to their PC problems.

Earning Money (including part-time work)

While co-op earnings will not pay all the costs of education for most students, they can make a nice dent in your expenses. Many internships are unpaid, but some offer stipends or at least modest salaries. Many students also have the opportunity to stay with their employer to work part-time hours after returning to classes. How much money you make will depend mainly on your field and your experience. For example, even an outstanding co-op student in early childhood education will make much less than the average student in accounting, engineering, or computer science. Also, it makes sense that a finance concentrator with no job experience and no coursework in the field will have much less earning power than an upperclassmen with classroom knowledge and co-op experience. As for part-time internships, it makes sense that someone doing a computer-related job is more likely to get a paid position than someone who wants to work in an aquarium or at a TV station or record company.

Your earnings as a co-op or intern also can be affected heavily by your flexibility. Having a car obviously will open up numerous opportunities for you versus the student who is stuck on public transportation. While this is true in all fields, it can be especially dramatic for some majors depending on where they are seeking a job. For marketing students at Northeastern, most of the good quality jobs are not incredibly far away with a car—but they are completely inaccessible by public transportation. Additionally, being open to the possibility of relocating to work out of state and/or being willing to work in a variety of areas also will increase your earning—and learning—potential. When you're competing against dozens of students who cannot or will not consider working out of state, you may find numerous terrific jobs and surprisingly little competition beyond the immediate reach of your university.

Other factors affecting earnings may include grades, the time of year that you choose to work, your effort in the job search (including effort in teaching yourself relevant skills), and soft skills such as communication skills, interpersonal skills, and attitude.

Return on your investment in education
Above all, real-world experience gives you a chance to get a nice return on the investment of time, money, and energy that you have put into your collegiate career. Studies have shown that full-time co-op students get a nice head start in terms of post-graduate earnings and quality of job opportunities. The more you strive to accomplish, the bigger the payoff at the end.

GETTING READY FOR A FUTURE REAL-WORLD EXPERIENCE

Maybe your first professional job experience is still a long way off. For some people reading this book, their first clinical or co-op or internship may be more than a year away. That's a long time, and there's no point in beginning a job search when your availability is in the distant future. Still, there are plenty of things that you can do *right now* to improve your chances of getting a better job when the time comes. But first, it's important to understand a critical question: What do employers *want* when they are looking to hire an intern, co-op candidate, or even a full-time hire coming right of college?

Common Fears
As stated earlier, about 90 percent of NU students who are admitted into our College of Business Administration cite co-op as their number-one reason for picking the program. However, many students still experience a good degree of fear and anxiety about beginning their co-op careers. This is natural: Most students recognize the value and importance of practical job experience but begin the program with limited knowledge about the job market and the co-op process as well as significant concerns about their lack of professional jobs in the past.

Very frequently, students meeting with their co-op coordinator for the first time express concerns about what their first co-op may hold: "No one will ever want to hire me—I have absolutely no corporate experience!" Believe me, we hear that one a lot. In fact, I would guess that probably two-thirds of our students begin the program without anything more than unskilled-labor positions on their resumes. Students also worry about the negative impact of poor grades, lack of a car, a sagging economy, and competition from other (presumably better) candidates.

The first thing to remember is that we want you to limit your fears and concerns to the things that you *can* control. You can worry about the economy, the job market, and how good other job candidates are—but in the end, worrying about these things won't change them at all.

Fortunately, there are quite a few things that you can control. You also may have more going for you than you realize, as you'll soon see.

What are employers seeking when hiring co-ops and interns?

When I first took over the MIS program in March 1995, my colleagues Bill Sloane and Charlie Bognanni suggested that I get out on the road to meet as many employers as possible in order to understand the needs of my program. It was great advice, and it yielded surprising information. I thought I already knew what MIS employers were seeking when they hired co-op students: computer skills, naturally! I expected employers to list applications: "Well, we want someone who can use Novell NetWare and who knows Visual Basic or another programming language...."

I did hear some employers say those kinds of things—but only about one-third of the time. Two times out of three, the manager would say something like this: "Computer skills are great—the more the better. But more than anything, we want someone who wants to be here every day, someone who thinks it's fun to learn new things, a hard worker who communicates well and gets along with people.... Someone who can work independently and show initiative but also work in a team... Someone who doesn't complain and moan and whine when something has to be done that's a little *less* fun. We'd much rather have a student who is weak on technical skills and strong in terms of these other qualities than to have it the other way around."

After hearing this several times, I asked a few managers to explain why they felt this way. "In six months, I can teach someone a lot about UNIX or Windows NT, assuming that they're smart and motivated," a manager said. "But I can't teach a person to want to come in to work every day."

Another manager flipped it around the other way. "If you haven't learned how to take pride in what you do, how to respect other people, and have a positive attitude in the first 18 years of your life," she mused, "then *how am I going to change all of that in just six months!*"

Even Microsoft—an employer that obviously features an extremely technical environment—basically follows this rule. Look at the following sidebar box, and consider the emphasis.

Hiring Co-ops and Interns – An Employer's Perspective
by Steve Sim
From a Microsoft perspective, it's difficult to specify anything in particular, but we look for the core competencies we wish all MS employees to possess:
- ◊ Passion for Technology
- ◊ Big Bold Goal Mentality
- ◊ Honest and Self-Critical
- ◊ Accountability
- ◊ Intelligence
- ◊ Team & Individual Achievement

Steve Sim is a Technical Recruiter at the Microsoft Corporation.

For most co-op students, this is extremely encouraging news: Students who want to be in a practice-oriented program requiring work generally have a strong work ethic. Most students I've met have at least some of those desirable soft skills. I have found—just as those managers had told me—that it is indeed very hard to change *who a person is* as opposed to changing their skill set. This attitude is not unique to MIS employers. Consider what one of our marketing employers has to say in this sidebar box:

Hiring Co-op Students – An Employer's Perspective
by Mike Naclerio
Energy and passion: You can teach a student or an employee the skills that are necessary for a position, but you cannot teach someone dedication and enthusiasm. If you build an organization based on quality people, you will get quality results.

Mike Naclerio is the Director of Relationship Management at the workplace HELPLINE.

This is not just true in business environments. Consider what one of our physical therapy co-op faculty told me when I asked her what her employers wanted in first-time professional hires:

What Employers Want – A Health Sciences Co-op Perspective
by Rose Dimarco
They're looking for someone who wants to learn, who's dependable, reliable, and who has some experience in a team environment—whether an athletic team or a debate team. Those are the things that they really are buying when you start school. When you graduate, they'll look more at technical skills, but they'll always be hiring professional behaviors. Always. That consists of how you perform in a "professional" environment.

Rose Dimarco is a cooperative education faculty coordinator in Physical Therapy at Northeastern University.

Even for students in highly technical disciplines, this holds true. Employers do want to see basic technical skills, but they are not the primary concern when hiring:

What Employers Want – An Engineering Co-op Perspective
by Bob Tillman

Does it look like you have the skills and abilities? Does it look like you have your head on straight, and does it look like you'll show up at work on time every day? Because we're going to teach you everything else. So the question is, does it look like you'll to fit in? Does it look like you have the entry-level skills so you know how to turn a computer on, you know how to plot in AutoCAD already, you know how to bring drawings up. We'll teach you everything else, but you need to look like you can learn. So you need to talk about being able to learn, being responsible, showing up, and doing the job.

Bob Tillman is a cooperative education faculty coordinator
in Civil Engineering at Northeastern University.

Of course, there are a few catches here. If possible, most typical managers would prefer to hire someone who has the soft skills AND some relevant technical skills—especially in a tough economy in which jobs are less plentiful. An inexperienced student who is a great person will not get a position if they're competing with great people who also have experience. Additionally, can't any snake oil salesman walk into an interview and *claim* to have a great attitude, excellent ability to work independently, and a terrific work ethic?? Absolutely. But there are steps you can take to change your skill set NOW and to help *prove* that you really have those soft skills, so let's consider those next.

Ways to improve your marketability before you start your job search

This has to be one of the most underutilized steps that you can take, and there's nothing to keep you from starting to do this right away—even if your next job search is not on the immediate horizon. Here's the key: start devoting some time toward improving your knowledge of your field. A criminal justice student could go out and do informational interviews with professionals in law enforcement and security. A veterinary science student would gain valuable experience and demonstrate a great deal about her interest in her field by volunteering at an animal shelter. For a finance student, this could mean reading *The Wall Street Journal* or *Smart Money* or any number of other periodicals or books that will help you understand stocks and bonds, mutual funds, investment philosophy, and concepts such as risk versus reward and the present value versus the future value of money. Just about any Information Technology student (whether majoring in computer science, engineering, or business) would benefit by picking up computer skills on their own—whether through using online tutorials, reading books such as *HTML for Dummies*, attending on-campus workshops on specific computer skills. Last year I worked with a student who had earned about five computer certifications on her own. This absolutely raised the eyebrows of potential employers. Likewise, taking meaningful courses in other majors such as Computer Science or English Composition instead of some bunny course to get an easy grade also can boost your technical skills and soft skills.

Improving Your Marketability – A Health Sciences Co-op Perspective
by Rose Dimarco

I'll tell you what you can do: Get the best possible understanding of yourself. When you're president of your class, or when you go and work in a camp job or as a waitress, start looking at what energizes you in that job and what doesn't. Once you know that, you can better assess what a better job is for you at co-op time. It's getting beyond 'I only want to work with children,' 'I only want to work with chronically ill people.' It has to do with understanding the role you play at that site: Does that site value what you bring to that role naturally? You're not going to have all the academically critical skills to do the job; everyone knows that. You're bringing *you*, and you have to be able to articulate who you are and what you can offer that environment. There's no such thing as a lousy job; there are just jobs that are incompatible with who you know you are.

Try to be around people who need health-care assistance. That can be an elderly grandmom; that could be a neighbor who has a child with some form of disability. That could be volunteering in a nursing home part-time, even working in a hospital gift shop: You're seeing families going through your gift shop on their way to see someone who is ill. Seeing how all that fits will take time, but there is a connection between the healing process that's underway on that floor and that conversation in the gift shop when that mom and dad were heading up to see their child, and what they did to try and make things better. I would say that any experience involving some sort of service can go on your resume, and employers will value students who have volunteered and have exposure to different areas.

Rose Dimarco is a cooperative education faculty coordinator
in Physical Therapy at Northeastern University.

Making the most of all on-campus resources

Most universities have tons of resources that you pay for with your tuition, whether or not you take advantage of them. Most universities and colleges have Departments of Career Services—featuring numerous resources that you may find valuable. You can research jobs in different fields, take tests that help you build self-awareness about how you might match up with different careers, and perhaps even have a practice interview videotaped and critiqued.

Your university library is a good source for periodicals relating to different fields, careers, and organizations. Most universities also have counseling centers—good places to go if personal problems are causing you difficulties, whether job-related or otherwise. Another little-known fact is that some counseling centers—such as the one at Northeastern—also can help with issues such as time management and test-taking anxiety.

Utilizing On-Campus Resources – An Arts & Sciences Co-op Perspective
by Ronnie Porter
We now encourage students to obtain part-time positions or internships over the summer to prepare themselves for getting their first co-op job. It would really depend on the field they're interested in. We might direct them to Career Services. There might be other resources on campus: we might direct them to the departments to check with faculty. We encourage them to really take advantage of their work-study positions, maybe working with a faculty member on research or some capacity like that to further develop their skills. We would really ask them to think about making the best use of any opportunities like that to develop their transferable skills.

Ronnie Porter is a cooperative education faculty coordinator
in Biology at Northeastern University.

Taking career-related courses

Increasingly, many universities are offering and even requiring career-related courses. Some—such as the excellent Gateway To The Workplace course at LaGuardia Community College in New York—are mandatory prerequisites to obtaining an internship or co-op job through the program. Given that these courses are often one-credit, pass-fail courses, some students might be tempted to go through the motions in these courses, doing just enough to get by. However, that would be a missed opportunity. These classes gives you a chance to get questions answered, undergo some career counseling, learn the fundamentals of resume writing and interviewing, and start to understand the logistics of how the co-op process works for you. It also can help you develop a good relationship with a co-op coordinator who can be a resource for you during all of your undergraduate years.

Start owning the responsibility for your success

One characteristic of interns and co-op students who are highly successful is that they own the responsibility for their success. In other words, a great co-op student is one who doesn't wait for things to happen but instead makes things happen for themselves. Just recently, a student came to see me ONE FULL MONTH after the official start date for his first co-op. Why did he blow off working with the co-op department? Well, a couple of friends had told him that the job market was tough and that he probably wouldn't be able to get a professional job. In talking to him, I quickly learned that he had good communication skills and a car. I had to tell him that basically 100 percent of our students with cars had been able to find related jobs in their majors—even in the bad economy. What a shame that he listened to people who knew little about the situation: Based on gossip and speculation from uninformed classmates, he went out on his own and got a job as a cashier in a restaurant. He looked absolutely sick when I told him that people with less going for them than him were making as much as $16/hour doing work directly related to their major!

Show some initiative as you plan ahead for your future co-op. When you interview for psychology job and are asked about some aspect of the field, you don't want to say "I don't know anything about that because we haven't covered it in class yet." Maybe you can talk about reading Irvin Yalom's excellent book *Love's Executioner*, which features remarkable tales of psychotherapy. Likewise, a journalism student should be able to cite *New York Times* articles that they thought to be excellent; a political science student should be able to speak—very diplomatically, of course—about pressing political issues in their city, state, or in the nation. Hiring managers look for results-oriented self-starters who don't sit back and wait for someone to force them to learn a new skill set or about relevant developments in the field.

A great deal will depend on your outlook. If you have negative expectations about your co-op or internship, you are more likely to focus on the negatives in your job. If you take the attitude that hard work, good performance, and a cheerful tone can overcome the negatives in most jobs, you probably will find that to be true. The key is to start taking small steps toward success.

Co-op Success Factors – A Student's Perspective
by Mark Moccia
A student should be active as soon as the college career begins. The key to landing the job you want is not throwing pennies into a fountain, hoping for the Gods of Co-op to "bestow the perfect job upon thee." A student must work hard to improve grades, add skills, participate in clubs, and take on other activities to show they are hard working and potential leaders.

Equally as important, a student must first decide their priorities before looking for a job. Some students might be looking to make good money, gain valuable experience, work for a large company, small company, etc. Once this is decided, the student then can begin to search for particular jobs.
Mark Moccia was an Accounting/MIS student at Northeastern University, Class of 2002

UNDERSTANDING THE JOB MARKET

As stated in the last section, you cannot control the nature of the economy, the job market, or cyclical factors that affect the quantity and quality of jobs available in your field. Yet although it does little good to fret about what you can't control, you still need to be aware of these elements and the impact they may have on your job search.

The economy
The United States economy is large, complex, hard to understand, and certainly impossible to change. Yet you should realize how this can affect you as an individual. Throughout the lives of most college students today, there have been very few economic crises in this country—especially during the last decade or so. However, it's naïve to think that the stock market and job market will always work in your favor.

Some students seeking jobs in 2001 and 2002 found out the hard way that this is the case. While there has not been rampant co-op unemployment, there certainly were fewer jobs available in many fields due to the sagging economy. A few co-op employers went bankrupt or laid off the majority of their workers; some co-op employers cut back their co-op headcount to some degree due to economic uncertainty.

The upshot has been that many students struggled to get jobs during these years, especially if they a) started their job search late, b) were inflexible about what type of job they were able and/or willing to do and where, geographically, they would or could work, or c) were inconsistent in their job-search efforts. Doing everything on time and to the best of your ability is no guarantee of getting a job in a challenging economy, but expending energy on the controllable part of your job search will help you fare better when grappling with something as uncontrollable as the US economy. *The amount of effort expended on the job search is the single biggest factor in determining whether or not an individual student is meaningfully employed or not—a much bigger factor than skills and job experience!* Most co-op and internship programs are NOT placement agencies—they don't simply assign you to a job; you have to earn it.

Even in a tough economy, it's also important to remember that there can be opportunities if you know where to look. According to Paul Harrington at the Center for Labor Market Studies at Northeastern University, full-time job seekers coming out of school in May 2003 may have fared best if they were willing to look at the Rocky Mountain region—especially given that New England had been losing quite a few jobs. Next year, the hot place for new hires after graduation may be the southwest, northwest—who knows? Again, the more you lock yourself into thinking that you MUST work in your local region, the more you are going to limit your options.

The job market in your field
Your chosen field will have a big impact on the quality and quantity of job options available to you. Although the economy also affects job markets—for example, computer science students had incredible options in the mid-nineties but struggled when the technology sector cooled off in 2001 and 2002—you will always be affected by the simple laws of supply and demand. 2002 and 2003 were great years for health science students in the Northeast—even though they were lean years for many other fields. If the demand in the job market for professionals in your field is greater than the supply of workers available, you may have some amazing options, even as an entry-level co-op student. But if you're in a field that is very popular with college students who are competing for a limited number of jobs, then it's a very different story.

Let's consider a few specific examples. Recently, it became more difficult for students to complete all of the requirements necessary to become Certified Public Accountants (CPAs). As a result, a significant number of students have drifted away from this concentration. Yet companies still need people to do accounting work, and accounting firms are still hiring at a healthy rate. The result is that accounting students now enjoy one of the best job markets amongst business students, as the supply of jobs is greater than the number of co-op students who are able and willing to fill them.

On the other side of the coin, there are always students who want to get into what I often call "sexy" jobs. A "sexy" job involves working in a field that individuals between the ages of 18 and 25 find to be glamorous. Imagine how many people in your age range want to work in the music industry, fashion, television, professional sports management, publishing, and advertising. Likewise, how many co-op students would want to work for organizations such as Reebok or the FBI or in the White House?

Given that so many students want to work in these fields or with these organizations, the result is that these employers often opt for students who will work for free as interns instead of hiring paid co-ops. If you really, really want to work in a "sexy" field, be prepared to work for little or nothing.... Or be creative about how you break into the field.

When I worked with NU's entrepreneurship students who wanted to get into sports management and who fantasized about working with the Boston Red Sox, I would tell them about my friend Tom Ford. Tom got his MBA and wanted to get into professional baseball, so he got the best job he could get to gain experience: He became a jack-of-all-trades for the Idaho Falls Braves—a very low-level minor league baseball team. Tom did everything from grooming the baseball field to taking tickets to picking out goofy sound effects to play over the loudspeaker when a foul ball left the park and went into the press box. He often worked 12+ hours a day for pitifully low wages. But within a few years he landed a dream position: general manager for a team in the high minor leagues in Tom's home state of Tennessee.

So you can break into glamorous fields if you're willing to pay the price in terms of time and money. The other way to do it is to acquire hot skills and use those skills as a way to differentiate yourself from other candidates. A few years ago I did a presentation on interviewing at a national co-op conference. Afterwards, two gentlemen from the CIA introduced themselves. Without any prompting from me, they said "Tell your students that if they want to work for the FBI and CIA, the way to do it is to major in computer science, MIS, or computer engineering. You have no idea how many criminal justice students contact us, and we're not interested in them!"

You always have to think about whom you're competing with for jobs and how you're going to be able to say, "I'm different!" We'll talk about that more in the interviewing chapter.

Time of year

Your ability to get the job of your choice also can be influenced by the time of year during which you hope to land that job. For business students at Northeastern, the two most common choices are to work for six months starting in early January or to work six months starting in mid-June. Our first-time students trying to pick one of the options always ask, "Which is a better choice?"

Basically, there are tradeoffs either way. There are more job opportunities available in early January because fewer students are available to work during that time of year—yet this also means that there is more competition from other NU students, and you also will need to be in school during the summer—which some students think is great but others don't like.

If you start co-op during the summer, you're competing with everyone else in the collegiate world who is seeking a summer job. Thus, there are fewer jobs available, but there are also fewer NU students seeking a job at that time. Working six months instead of as a summer-only worker gives you an edge over students from conventional programs, so that helps, too.

As we saw when considering "sexy" jobs, what you want to avoid is doing what everyone else does. Again, how can you differentiate yourself from other candidates? For example, the worst thing you can do as an NU student is look for a summer-only job: Then you're competing with every other college student PLUS all of the NU students who can work for six months. Ugh! Not recommended.

Your chosen field also may have a different supply of jobs at different times of the year. About two-thirds of our accounting students choose to be on co-op for the first six months of the year due to tax season. This is a win-win situation because organizations can get help for their busy season and not have to pay for year-round people who won't be necessary during the summer and fall. Meanwhile, students get to work in action-packed jobs, which are always preferable to slow-paced work environments.

Having realistic expectations

This is especially true for first-time co-op students. We sometimes meet with nursing students who think that their first job as a nursing co-op will entail providing direct care for patients—even though their background is limited to prerequisite courses in anatomy and physiology. Then there is the entrepreneurship student who wants to own a restaurant some day and thus gets a job in a restaurant, believing that she will be making decisions about the menu. Or the computer science student who believes he will be a key member of a software development team, taking the lead in designing a new software application for the company. Wrong, wrong, and wrong!

No company in their right mind is going to hand major decision-making power to a business intern or co-op student who has not even taken a single course in finance or marketing! Legally, health care providers have to be very careful about what they allow co-ops, interns, and clinical students to do. For American Sign Language students, most job opportunities require fully trained professionals with degrees. As a result, the best that an ASL co-op or intern may be able to hope for is a position that provides them with informal opportunities to practice their ASL skills with deaf people, rather than a role in which he or she is an "official translator."

More than anything, your first co-op is a great opportunity to gain initial exposure to the professional world in the field of your choice—just "being around" in that kind of environment can be a good learning experience, even if your job duties entail monotonous Quality Assurance software testing to find and document programming bugs or chopping vegetables up at a restaurant or being a "sitter" in hospital: basically sitting by a patient in an Intensive Care Unit for hours to make sure that they don't pull any of their tubes out (all possible duties for the students mentioned in the previous paragraphs).

Co-op students need to work their way up the ladder by proving themselves in whatever role they are given. Repeatedly in this book, you will hear about how co-op success—versus mere survival or outright failure—is all about *momentum*. Co-ops and interns are often given low-level tasks when starting a new position. Why? Employers want to see what you can do, and they often want to give you tasks that you can handle to build confidence and start off successfully.

If you take on these low-level tasks cheerfully and efficiently, you may find that you are suddenly being asked to take on more and better projects. Fail to do them with the right attitude or without success, and you are less likely to get more advanced work to do. Having realistic expectations about your first job will enable you to approach the job with a good attitude—an understanding that you may need to work your way up in the organizational world.

JOB SEARCH OPTIONS

At a large institution, it is very unlikely that a co-op, internship, or career services coordinator will hold your hand throughout the job search process. At NU, we do a great deal for some of our students—generally the ones who are planning ahead, putting considerable energy into their co-op careers, and actively seeking our guidance and direction. However—given the size of our student loads—we just don't have enough hours in the day to call you up regularly during placement season to ask why you haven't come in with your resume. It's really up to you to be on top of what you need to get done and when you have to do it in terms of the placement process.

Working with a co-op or internship coordinator and/or career services department

If your university has a co-op/internship coordinator or career services department, by all means take advantage of these resources. At schools with established programs, these career professionals are the liaison to hundreds, even thousands, of jobs. The co-op/internship or career services coordinator should have a good understanding of the specifics of the job market in your field and region. Plus, he or she talks to hundreds of employers about their employment needs. If you don't work with a coordinator, you won't have access to all kinds of information!

The best advice I can give you regarding working successfully with your co-op or career services coordinator is to treat this individual in the same way that you would treat your supervisor in the workplace. Use your interactions with co-op coordinators as opportunities to hone your professionalism.

What does this mean in practical terms?

- When meeting a coordinator for the first time, introduce yourself, shake hands, and clearly state your reasons for the office visit.

- Be on time to appointments with these professionals. If you absolutely cannot make an appointment, call in advance to cancel instead of just being a no-show.

- Be sensitive to the coordinator's need to juggle multiple priorities on a tight time schedule.

- When faced with uncertainty, assume the best: For example, if your coordinator asks you to change your resume, assume that it's with your best interests in mind, not to inconvenience you!

- If you need to state concerns or air conflicts, try to do so in an upbeat, solution-oriented way rather than simply blowing off steam or complaining.

- When in doubt about what you should do in *any* situation—before, during, or after you obtain your job—ask your coordinator.

It's definitely in your best interest to develop a good working relationship with your coordinator. Inevitably, when great new jobs come in, we think first about the students whom we know well and who are in touch with us regularly. With large student loads, students can easily fall off our radar screens. Stay in touch regularly to make sure that doesn't happen, and you likely will be the beneficiary of a wealth of good advice and assistance in the job search process. "I just haven't had time" or "You're not available at times that are convenient to me" just don't cut it as excuses—it only takes a minute or two to write an e-mail or leave a voice mail with an update. More often than not, your coordinator also can make accommodations to meet with you if the posted appointment times or walk-in hours don't correspond well with your availability.

Finding A Job On Your Own

Some students may find it useful or even absolutely necessary to find a job without much help from their college or university. Some schools don't have formal co-op or internship coordinators or programs. Even if you go to a big co-op school, you may want to look for your own job for various reasons. A Northeastern student seeking a job in his home state may need to find her own job—especially if the desired job is outside of New England, southern New York, or New Jersey. You also may need to or want to find your own job if you are seeking work in a field that your co-op department typically doesn't work with. Examples might be some of those "sexy" fields that were mentioned earlier in this chapter: music industry, fashion, sports management, and advertising come to mind.

Although your job search falls outside of the conventional paths available through your school, you still have options. However, there are a few things to bear in mind before striking out on your own:

1. *Always check with your co-op or internship coordinator before approaching any companies.* If you have a connection with IBM, for example—even one through a classmate, friend, or family member—it would be a mistake to approach the company without getting clearance from your co-op coordinator first. The reason is that your school may have already established a co-op relationship with them, and both IBM and the co-op department may perceive you as trying to "beat the system" or do an "end run" instead of legitimately following the process as other students do. In some cases, you may need to discuss your job lead with the appropriate co-op coordinator before making contact to avoid any misunderstandings.

2. *You must get your co-op coordinator's approval before accepting any job found on your own, and you must get that approval BEFORE the beginning of the work experience.* Not all jobs qualify as co-op positions. For many students at Northeastern, the jobs must be full-time positions (Minimum 35 hours/week) and they must be appropriate to your career; other programs may be more flexible and less strict about what qualifies as a co-op, but you need to be sure. Also, your coordinator is responsible for knowing your whereabouts on co-op and for submitting data on your salary to the university administration. In most programs, coordinators simply will not give a student credit for a work experience if they fail to discuss the position with her or him beforehand—even if the student obtained a fantastic position on his own.

3. *Even though you are pursuing your own job, don't forget that your co-op coordinator can be very helpful to you in your job search.* Sometimes coordinators can give students job leads depending on their circumstances, and most coordinators can help with resumes, cover letters, networking tips, and advice on how to sell the idea of co-op to an organization. Take advantage of this resource. Also note that Appendix C in the back of this book has information on how to write a cover letter. You would be amazed at how many

long-time professionals really have no idea how to write cover letters effectively. Learn now!

4. *Be sure to complete the appropriate paperwork with your co-op coordinator.* Have a copy of an agreement form (or any other paperwork required by your school) ready to fill out and give it to your coordinator upon locating a suitable position.

Coming Up With Job Options On Your Own

For most students, one of the most challenging parts of finding their own co-op job is managing to get in the door for interviews. After all, co-op employers don't usually put co-op job listings in the newspaper or on a job board. The trick is becoming more creative about how you come up with options. Here are some suggestions:

1. *Network through family and friends.* As stated earlier, don't use family and friends to get to employers that already work with your school's co-op program—discuss this step with your co-op coordinator first. After clearing that hurdle, you'll find that networking is the single most effective way of finding your own job.

   An entrepreneurship/small business management student of mine a few years ago came to see me and announced that she wanted to find a job in Denver. She had a cousin who lived there but otherwise knew no one in Colorado. Together, we worked hard on how to network. Armed with that knowledge, she began grilling her cousin: Whom do you know who works in a small business? Where do they work? What's their phone number? When she found people who worked in small businesses, she tried to get them thinking about her situation: Could your company use someone to work on marketing projects? Someone to help with computers? An individual who could crunch numbers, work as a good team player, and serve as a Jill-of-all-trades?

   Even though she experienced a lot of rejection, the student stayed positive, upbeat, and persistent—to the point where people really *wanted* to help her find a job. Plus she tried to avoid any dead ends: Anyone she talked to was an opportunity to get more names and phone numbers. Finally, she got a fantastic job, working for a small business that helped other businesses put together IPOs and go public. How many people did she have to go through to make this happen? The job was obtained through her cousin's boyfriend's father's friend's friend!!! It just shows what you can do if you are willing to expend some energy in an intelligent, directed search for your own job.

2. *Check out job boards and newspaper listings.* At Northeastern, many undergraduates can use HuskyCareerLink, which NU students access by going to northeastern.erecruiting.com on the Web. Hundreds of employers list jobs through HuskyCareerLink, and many schools now have similar sites that are worth checking. Some employers are purely interested in hiring full-time

employees who have completed their degrees (or who will do so very soon), while others can be approached about co-ops or internships and are interested in forging bonds with the university. Some even list temporary or hourly positions that might be very appropriate for a student seeking a co-op job.

Beyond that, there are numerous job boards out there: If you go to careers.altavista.com, you'll find links to about ten of them. A few include monster.com, brainbuzz.com, and USJobBoard.com. Some sites are extremely national and general, while others focus more on specific fields and regions: For example, dice.com features high tech jobs.

Bear in mind that most employers list full-time jobs on these boards—not co-op jobs or internships. Therefore, undergrads probably won't be successful at targeting specific listed jobs. Instead, the job boards will give you some indication of who is looking to hire in your field. Chances are that an employer hiring significant numbers of full-time employees may view a co-op program as another good (if longer-term) recruiting option.

Of course, sometimes organizations listing multiple jobs on the boards are actually employment agencies, which generally are not interested in placing co-op students. While these may be useful for those of you seeking your first full-time job after graduation, co-op and internship seekers probably should steer clear of them at this point in their careers.

Most of the same rules apply for newspaper listings. One good thing to know, though, is that many newspapers also have their classified jobs online. You can save a lot of time by searching for key words in online listings as opposed to reading thousands of ads in the Sunday paper!

3. *Making Cold Calls.* Telephoning, e-mailing, or stopping in at an employer is a last resort because you will put in a lot of energy without much return in many cases. You can improve your chances by targeting larger employers, checking whether there is information about co-op jobs on their website, and then getting in touch to express your interest.

Selling A Company On The Value Of A Co-op Employee
One of the best things about finding your own job is that it is a great way to test your ability to be entrepreneurial. You have to not only sell yourself in the interview as you ordinarily would: Often you will need to be able to articulate how cooperative education works and why it benefits potential employers. Here are some key points to hit:

1. *Co-op employees and interns represent cost-effective labor.* In many cases— especially with corporate jobs—these employees are a less expensive resource than the alternatives, such as contractors or temps.

21

2. *Co-ops/interns do not need to receive benefits.* Health care benefits and paid vacation time are expensive to employers; many companies are under pressure to keep their "headcount" (full-time employees who are eligible for benefits) at a minimum. Co-ops and interns are one way to help achieve this goal. Note that co-ops are NOT contractors: state and federal taxes DO need to be withdrawn from your pay.

3. *Co-ops/interns can provide long-term help but are not a permanent commitment.* If you can make yourself available for six months, that's a long time: long enough for you to provide a return on the investment the company may need to make in training you. However, the company need not make any commitment beyond the six months to you or other co-op students or interns. This may be important to start-up companies, which may need help now but are unsure about what their future needs may be. Likewise, even large employers may be reluctant to commit to a permanent hire during times of economic uncertainty. Hiring a co-op or intern for three to six months is far preferable to hiring a full-time employee without knowing if they will need to lay off the person in the next year. Better still, when the economy turns around, these programs mean that the organization has been able to maintain a recruiting pipeline.

4. *Interns and co-op students have much at stake and are therefore more motivated than other temporary workers usually are.* People who work as temps usually do so simply to make money. Co-op student workers usually focus on learning as much as they can and securing a good reference for future employment. As a result, co-ops often show more interest and effort in their jobs.

Your coordinator may be able to provide you with an introductory brochure about co-ops and interns for potential employers and other materials that may be useful to you in marketing yourself as a temporary student/employee.

Now that you have a good understanding of how to plan ahead for your first professional job, you are ready to tackle the nuts and bolts of the preparation stage: writing a resume, learning how to interview, and generally ramping up for your job search.

Chapter 1 Review Questions

1. Name at least four of the benefits of working as a co-op or intern.

2. List three things that you could do now to make yourself more marketable for a future position in your field.

3. Why do many hiring managers consider soft skills more important than technical skills when hiring co-ops, interns, or graduating seniors?

4. What are two specific things that you could do to prove to a future interviewer that you are willing and able to learn quickly?

5. What does the text describe as the single biggest factor in determining whether or not an individual student is meaningfully employed or not?
   A. The economy
   B. The job market in your field
   C. Skills and Experience
   D. Amount of effort expended in the job search
   E. Flexibility, including willingness to relocate

6. Name at least three ways in which co-ops and internships are beneficial to employers.

CHAPTER TWO
Writing An Effective Resume

INTRODUCTION

Your resume is a vital component of an effective job search. It is a personal statement and advertisement of who you are. You may have more talent, knowledge and skills than any other applicant for a particular job. However, if you don't get an opportunity to communicate those qualities to an employer, you may never get the chance to demonstrate your abilities. A good resume will provide you with that opportunity. It WILL NOT get you a job but it CAN get you an interview.

As you will see in this chapter, there are different schools of thought on how resumes should be written. Some co-op and internship coordinators or career services professionals believe that resume writers should go beyond describing simply what they did to weave in soft skills portrayed in previous work experience. Alternatively, your co-op coordinator may encourage you to put some "spin" on your job descriptions—encouraging you to describe *how* you did a given job or what made you a good or great employee in a given position. That will help a potential employer *infer* what soft skills you have. However, other co-op coordinators believe that it's best to emphasize what you did and not force the potential employer to wade through a long-winded job description. From this perspective, the idea is to use the interview to convey your soft skills and anything more qualitative that the interviewer may want to know about your previous positions. Some employers believe that resumes are somewhat overrated (see the sidebar box on top of the next page).

Resume Writing – An Employer's Perspective
by Mike Naclerio
Not much impresses me on resumes. I don't spend much time reviewing them and view them as a mere formality. The personal interview is what counts, and where you can truly determine whether an individual will fit into your unique working environment.
Mike Naclerio is the Director of Relationship Management at the workplace HELPLINE.

Conversely, some employers believe resumes are critically important. This type of employer may not call a student in because of a careless typo or a poorly organized resume. There is definitely no one "right" way to prepare resumes. Employers, family members, friends, co-op coordinators, professors, and recruiters often have strong opinions on the subject—and you'll find that they don't necessarily agree with each other! For example, some people believe that an Interests section is completely meaningless: yet I also have had more than one employer tell me that they can't imagine why anyone would be foolish enough to exclude an Interests section from their resume.

Your best bet is to find out what your co-op or career services professional believes would work best for you, given your work history as well as your field. You also need to think about what feels right and comfortable for YOU, Maybe your brother's girlfriend thinks you should do your resume a different way—the approach that *she* used in getting some fantastic job—or your mom is an HR manager who sees hundreds of resumes per year and believes she knows what is best for you. In the end, though, your co-op coordinator is the one who has dozens of co-op jobs available, whereas your brother's girlfriend probably doesn't have any! Make sure your coordinator understands your goals and values—are you comfortable, for example, with a resume that really sells your skills? Once your coordinator knows you, trusting that person's judgment is usually the best move.

Although there are various perspectives on how to write an effective resume, just about any professional would agree on many factors that differentiate a strong resume from a poor one. An effective, competitive resume is one that highlights your best achievements, accomplishments, and contributions at work, at school, and in the community. It also can reflect your hobbies, interests, and background, making you into a three-dimensional person instead of a name on a page. A strong resume also must be *flawless* in terms of typos or errors—after all, if you can't get things right on your resume, why would anyone expect you to have excellent attention to detail as an employee?

In contrast, a mediocre resume will provide minimal work and academic history plus extremely basic job descriptions. Also, a poor resume is unattractive to look at—maybe it's hard to read due to small type or poor alignment, perhaps it is just very inconsistent in terms of formatting. A weak resume also will have poor grammar or outright errors on it: failure to abbreviate properly, misspelled or misused words, or significant omissions. Employers often go through dozens of resumes in search of a handful of interview candidates. If you want your resume to stand out positively from the rest of the pile, you need to invest considerable time and thought. Therefore to learn how to write a winning, professional resume, read on!

Resume Writing – A Student's Perspective
by Mark Moccia
It has been said by many that your first impression is a lasting one. The resume is the first impression a student leaves on an employer and is critical in determining their chances of receiving an interview/position. A student with a bad resume is similar to a house with a faulty foundation; without the proper strength and support in the early phases, the final product will be less appealing. The resume is a perfect opportunity for the students to capture themselves and "wow" the employers with one sheet of paper. Simply put, a resume of poor quality will make the job search extremely difficult for the student.
Mark Moccia was an Accounting/MIS student at Northeastern University, Class of 2002

WRITING YOUR RESUME

The first step in writing your resume is easy. It has to do with the way your resume will look when it is finished. Remember, appearance does create a strong first impression. Just as you would not go to an interview dressed in a t-shirt and shorts, your resume also needs to look professional. The following five tips will help you to have a "good-looking" resume.

FIVE RESUME TIPS

- As a co-op student, your resume generally should be only ONE page in length on 8 1/2 X 11 inch bond paper.

- Use neutral colors when selecting bond paper (white, ivory, off-white, gray).

- It is recommended that you type your own resume on a word processor and save it on disk. This will enable you to make changes and corrections at any time. Also, most students will need to upload their resume onto the school's computer system and/or give an electronic copy of their resume to their coordinator.

- Almost everyone uses Microsoft Word when writing their resume, and 90 percent of resumes seem to use Word's default font—Times New Roman—as a result. Dare to be different! Experiment with other fonts (as long as they're not too wild). Arial is one reliable alternative... and there are many others such as Bell MT, Garamond, and Helvetica.

- Your resume should reflect you as a professional and as an individual—do not directly copy from the sample resumes in this chapter. Employers have commented on how too many resumes look exactly alike. Write your own!

Resume Writing – A Student's Perspective
by Keith Laughman

One of the greatest attributes of this book is its coverage on resume building. The first time someone writes a resume he or she might be too humble to beef themselves up. A resume is a marketable representation of who you are; it's the first and sometimes only impression that employers see of you. You want to create a sharp image in their eye and leave an imprint on their mind when they are done looking at your resume. This is what sets you apart from everybody else and this is why Northeastern is number one with its co-op program.

Throughout your lifetime, you will be revising your resume constantly. It's important to put a lot of energy into developing it for the future. Students should understand that a good resume takes time and thought. The process of building a resume is also a great opportunity for the student to learn more about themselves and how they have dealt with certain people and situations in the past, thus preparing them for the next big step, the interview.

Creating a resume was actually a fun experience for me. It helped me realize that I did much more at work than I thought and that although I had few skills relevant to my major, I had many interpersonal skills. These skills are just as effective as technical skills. Technical skills can be learned; you may have interpersonal skills, but they need to be developed! Four years later and I am still using the co-op guidebook as a resource to improve and refine my skills.

Keith Laughman was an MIS/Marketing Student at Northeastern University, Class of 2002

SECTIONS

Your resume will be broken down into a number of separate sections, which will be used to describe aspects of your life and qualifications. Every co-op resume should include sections on:

- Education
- Experience
- Skills

Depending on your background, you also might include several other possible sections, such as Interests, Military Experience, Volunteer Experience, Memberships, Major Accomplishments and Professional Certificates or Licenses.

HOW TO START

Every resume should start with an introduction. When you meet someone for the first time, you always tell them your name. Your resume is the same. Your name should be at the top, either centered, left or right—whichever you think fits best. Address, telephone numbers, and e-mail address are critical. Employers need to reach you should they want to interview you or make you an offer! Therefore, include a permanent (family) and temporary (local) address if they are different. Remember, your resume may stay on file for over a year with an employer while you move in the meantime. Your permanent address and telephone number will ensure that you can always be reached for a job offer. Likewise, you always want to include a reliable e-mail address that you check regularly. If you're always having trouble with your Hotmail or Yahoo account because you exceed the storage limit for messages, you need to do something to make sure that that won't happen to a potential employer.

Also, it's advisable to make sure that the number and address you want employers to call first is on the left-hand side, as they are most likely to use that one.

For example:

JANE SMITH
Janesmith73@hotmail.com

CURRENT ADDRESS   PERMANENT ADDRESS
7 Speare Hall, Box 00   89 Fifth Avenue
Boston, MA 02115   Natick, MA 01760
(617) 377-0000   (508) 555-0001

International students who use an Americanized nickname can include that on their resume. It could look like this:

WAI MAN 'Tony" LAM

What if you have an extremely difficult to pronounce name and are afraid that an employer may be reluctant to call you as a result? Recently, we heard of one enterprising student who included the pronunciation of his name right below it. You could do that like so:

OLUMIDE NGUNDIRI
(first name pronounced "oh-LOO-mee-day")
olumide@yahoo.com

EDUCATION

While you are still an intern cooperative education student, the education section is usually listed first. Upon graduation, this section often moves below the EXPERIENCE section. When writing the education section, you should use the following guidelines:

- Format: reverse chronological order (current university listed first, other universities and colleges second, high school last)

- Include anticipated degree (i.e., Bachelor of Science Degree in Business Administration; Bachelor of Arts Degree in English) and expected month and year of graduation

- Include concentrations and dual concentrations or minors, if applicable

- Honors: include GPA if 3.0 or above and any scholarships received (Compute your GPA to no more than two decimal places: 3.45 is fine; 3.4495 does not indicate greater honesty or make any significant difference to an employer)

- Include activities related to the University; leadership roles

- Include the above information for transfer schools

- If you are financing a significant portion of your education yourself, you may want to include that fact. For example:

Financing 80% of college tuition and expenses through cooperative education and part-time job earnings.

Here's how the section might look:

EDUCATION

NORTHEASTERN UNIVERSITY   Boston, MA
Bachelor of Science Degree in Business Administration   May 2007
Dual Concentration: Marketing and Finance
Minor: Communications
Grade Point Average: 3.2
Activities and Honors: University Honors Program, Joe Smith Memorial
Scholarship, Intramural Basketball, Residential Life Representative, Outing
Club
Financing 75% of tuition and living expenses through cooperative education earnings and part-time job income.

Many students who have not yet had significant work experience will find it helpful to include their high school education in this section. Since your resume is written in reverse chronological order, the recording of your high school experience would come AFTER your university or college notation.

EXPERIENCE

This is the most vital section of your resume. This is the time not only to list where you worked and what you did, but to list your accomplishments and achievements! Take time to think about what you want to say—it's worth doing right! Here are some key points:

- *Include company name (the official name), location, job title, and dates of employment.* Employers want to see this information in order to determine exactly what you have done and how long you spent doing it. They might use this information to contact your present or previous employer in order to find out more about the relevance of your experience and the accuracy of your statements. Note that you probably shouldn't bother listing a job if you only did it for a month or two: Fairly or unfairly, it may raise questions about your ability and willingness to keep a job.

- *Jobs should be listed chronologically from present position, then backwards.* List your present or most recent position first, then your second most recent and so on. As you go through your university years, you probably will be getting more and more advanced jobs. If you have already had two internships jobs related to your major, for example, you certainly wouldn't want it to look like your waitressing job in high school was your most important experience to date. One exception to this rule: If your most recent job experience was not related to your major—for example, a part-time waitering job that you did while attending classes—you might want to have a section called "Relevant Job Experience" or "Internship Experience" *first*, followed by another section called "Other Job Experience" or "Part-time Job Experience," etc.

- *Sentences should always begin with an action verb.* Avoid starting sentences with weak linking verbs such as had, got, did, etc. Use verbs that convey confidence, such as handled, improved, managed, designed, etc. There is a long list of great action verbs toward the end of this chapter. An alternative is to start with a compelling adverb: "*Effectively* handled....", "*Successfully* managed...", etc.

- *Do not underestimate the power of word choice: Use power words, not passive words.* For example, don't say "Got information on orders for people who asked for it." Instead, say "Responded effectively to customer and colleague requests by tracking order status on computer and over the telephone."

- *Do not use personal pronouns such as "I," "me," "we" or "them".* On a resume, this amounts to stating the obvious. If your name is on the top of the resume, the reader knows that the statements refer to you unless you state otherwise.

- *Never begin a sentence with "Responsibilities included..." or "Duties include...".* This type of beginning may capture *what* you did, but you need to go further than that. Starting with action verbs helps you capture what you did and *how* you did it.

- *Quantify and qualify whenever possible.* For example: "Increased sales by 15%," or "Increased sales significantly by using suggestive-selling techniques." Either of these statements tells the reader much more about precisely how well you did or how you went about accomplishing this task. This is far preferable to simply writing "Sold products." Notice how much more powerful the following descriptions are when the large, bold-type descriptive part of the sentence is added:

  - Owned and operated snowplowing business **grossing $3,500 a winter**

  - Hired and supervised **five** employees

  - **Using Harvard Graphics**, created a **750-page color** presentation for the annual sales meeting

- *Highlight transferable skills.* Write your job descriptions in such a way that potential employers can see how your experience might make you a better candidate for a professional position. *This is especially true for job seekers who have NO experience in their chosen field.* Think of it this way: Let's say you're a human resource management concentrator who has never worked in a corporate environment. Perhaps the only jobs on your resume are working as a waiter and as a house painter. In all probability, you will not want to wait on tables or paint houses as a co-op employee. Therefore, most co-op coordinators—but not all—believe that it's helpful to include transferable skills on your resume.

How can you identify what your transferable skills are? Ask yourself two questions: Were you good at the job you did? If so, why? Was it because you managed to figure out how to do the job well in a short time (**ability to learn quickly**)? Your ability to keep customers happy (**customer-service skills** or maybe **interpersonal skills**)? Was it that you never missed work or showed up late (**dependability** or **strong work ethic** or **positive attitude**)?

The transferable skills that you choose to highlight will depend heavily on your concentration and the type of co-op job that is being sought. As my co-op colleague Rose Dimarco points out in the following sidebar box, it also depends very much on what purpose the resume needs to serve. If you're in a co-op or internship program in which the coordinator arranges the interview schedule for the employer, this calls for a very different resume compared to a situation in which the resume must get you in the door!

Tailoring Your Resume – A Health Sciences Co-op Perspective
by Rose Dimarco

A resume initially gives you a script. When you think about what you're willing to put on paper about yourself, it typically reflects how you're going to explain yourself. So are we talking about a resume that's going to *introduce* you, or is it going to be a *leave-behind* that is going to help an employer remember you and differentiate you from someone else? It might introduce you and that may the only decision-maker that they have to determine whether they call you for an interview, and that might adjust your resume somewhat. I'm just concerned that you're not boastful; that it's factual, but you also give yourself credit for what you've done.

If transferable skills are things that you feel are of value, that's what I would help you put on a resume in such a way that the interviewer reading it would conclude those things that you know about yourself: That you're a hard worker; that you're flexible—you don't necessarily want to use those terms on a resume, but you want them to conclude that from reading it. That's the art of resume writing in general, but in health care those are the things that we want to bring to the surface.

Rose Dimarco is a cooperative education faculty coordinator in Physical Therapy at Northeastern University.

Look at the list at the end of this chapter for a more complete list of transferable skills for the various majors and concentrations.

Certain verbs are very helpful to know when capturing transferable skills. Some good examples are displayed, demonstrated, utilized, exhibited, showed, and used. Often you can start out a job description sentence using one of these verbs and an appropriate adjective in front of a transferable skill. For example:

- Demonstrated excellent interpersonal skills when....

- Utilized solid communication skills when...

- Displayed outstanding ability to learn quickly while...

A "transferable skill cheat sheet" toward the end of this chapter has lists of these verbs and a summary of this transferable skill formula.

Note that you need to be a little careful about throwing transferable skills around. The worst thing you can do is to just mention these skills and leave out anything about what you actually did on the job. Employers need to know what you actually did—even if it was simply mopping floors or washing dishes! Also, be careful not to overuse the transferable skills—working one or two them into each job description may be adequate. Above all, NEVER claim that you have a certain transferable skill unless you are confident that you really have that skill—and that your former employer would agree. At worst, overemphasizing the transferable skills may come off as "BS" to some employers—especially if they believe that you're using them as smokescreen to hide the low level of what you really did. Calling a garbage collector a "sanitation engineer" doesn't change the nature of that smelly job. Likewise, it can come off as insincere overkill if you say "Demonstrated outstanding ability to learn quickly when maintaining lawns." How hard is it, really, to learn how to mow a lawn? In that case, it might be better to keep it simple: "Efficiently mowed lawns for neighborhood customers."

Resumes – An Employer's Perspective
by Myretta Robens
In a co-op resume, we mostly just look to see that it is neat and grammatically correct. Experience is not essential. In fact, one of my favorite resumes included the line, "Demonstrated a positive attitude while cleaning out horse stalls." I figured that if Sara could do that, she could handle anything our users threw at her. And that turned out to be the case.

Myretta Robens was the Director of Technology Operations at Harvard Business School Publishing.

- *Take time to think about how your job/contribution fits into the "big picture."* When capturing your job experience on a resume, don't just think about what tasks you did each day. Instead, consider the importance of these tasks with relation to what helped the organization accomplish its goals. For example: Don't just say, "Created window displays." Instead, show how your work made a small but important difference for your employer: "Generated customer interest by creating innovative window displays."

- *Either the bullet/outline format or the paragraph format is acceptable.* When writing up your job description, use which works best for you. If your job experience is complex and relatively hard to explain, the paragraph format may work best. If you had numerous and highly varied job responsibilities, you might find the bulleted format easier to use. It's up to you.

- *Volunteer experience can be included under EXPERIENCE or in a separate section.* Although you can be flexible about where to include volunteer experience, just make sure that you don't fail to include it somewhere on your resume. Working as a volunteer can show concern for others as well as a desire to learn through unpaid experience.

- *In most cases, write out numbers below 11.* Unless you're writing about percentages (e.g., 5%), you generally should write out numbers from one through ten (e.g., "Utilized two database programs"); higher numbers are written numerically (e.g., "Generated 75 leads for potential sales").

Remember, the Experience section usually is what a potential employer studies to make a preliminary decision about whether you can do the job. An ordinary description means you are an ordinary person. Now is the time to show an employer that you are extraordinary. The following are some helpful hints on how to do that.

A STEP-BY-STEP APPROACH TO WRITING UP YOUR JOB EXPERIENCE

Writing job descriptions takes time, effort, and practice. But once you learn how to do this effectively, you will have mastered a skill that will be useful to you for the rest of your career. Let's look at a step-by-step formula to writing effective job descriptions. Note that the changes in each step are indicated by having the text underlined: You would not actually underline any job description text on a real resume.

In the interest of giving equal time to two different perspectives, the first example will incorporate transferable skill phrases; the second will show how to write a job description without touting your soft skills.

Step 1
Write down the organization's name and location, then the job title and dates of employment on the second line:

SANTA'S TREE FARM	Kent, CT
Laborer	November 2001 - Present

Step 2
Write down in simple terms the various duties you had in a given job, like this:

SANTA'S TREE FARM	Kent, CT
Laborer	November 2001 - Present

- Plant trees and help them grow
- Mow property.
- Cut down trees for customers, accept payment, and tie trees to customers' cars.

Step 3
Add details describing the nature of the employer in question and the purpose of the job:

SANTA'S TREE FARM   Kent, CT
Laborer   November 2000 - Present
- <u>Working as only hired employee for small family-owned business</u>, plant trees and help them grow <u>to ensure that adequate supply of Christmas trees is available each winter.</u>
- Mow property <u>regularly to make sure that trees have adequate exposure to sunlight and room to grow.</u>
- Cut down trees for customers, accept payment, and tie trees to their cars.

Step 4
Add quantitative details and professional terms when possible to bring the experience to life:

SANTA'S TREE FARM   Kent, CT
Laborer   November 2000 - Present
- Working as only hired employee for small family-owned business, plant <u>over 300 trees annually</u> and help them grow to ensure that adequate supply of Christmas trees is available each winter.
- Mow property regularly to make sure that <u>all four varieties of evergreen</u> trees have adequate exposure to sunlight and room to grow.
- Cut down <u>approximately 200 trees per year</u> for customers, accept payment, and tie trees to their cars.

Step 5 (Optional)
Add phrases containing transferable skills in order to capture how well you did the job and what you might be able to provide to a co-op employer in a more professional setting:

SANTA'S TREE FARM   Kent, CT
Laborer   November 2000 - Present
- Working as only hired employee for small family-owned business, <u>exhibited an outstanding work ethic</u> when planting over 300 trees annually and helping them grow to ensure that adequate supply of Christmas trees is available each winter.
- <u>Demonstrated strong attention to detail</u> when mowing property regularly to make sure that all four varieties of evergreen trees have adequate exposure to sunlight and room to grow.
- <u>Displayed sense of responsibility and excellent customer-service skills</u> when cutting down approximately 200 trees per year for customers, accept payment, and tie trees to their cars.

By crafting this type of job description, a student shows a potential employer that they have many qualities that might be highly desirable in a co-op employee. Again, note that the inclusion of transferable skills is generally considered critical when you seek your first co-op jobs. As you advance in your career and obtain jobs that are directly related to your course of study, the explicit use of transferable skills becomes less important. But if you fail to include them when you do not have highly relevant job experience, you are asking an employer to make a real leap in terms of figuring out whether you have any qualities that might be useful to her or him.

ANOTHER EXAMPLE OF THIS STEP-BY-STEP APPROACH

One of the great advantages of using this step-by-step approach is that it will make your interview easier. If you take the time to nail down an excellent description of your job and employer, then that becomes one less thing that you will need to worry about accomplishing during the interview itself... when you won't have much time to think about what to say! Instead of having to explain the basics of your previous experience, you can build on the resume by diving into specific examples of the points made on your resume.

Let's consider another step-by-step example, leaving out the transferable skill formula this time around:

Step 1
Write down the organization's name and location, then the job title and dates of employment on the second line:

FENWAY PROJECT ADMINISTRATIVE OFFICE	Boston, MA
Office Assistant	April 1999-Present

Step 2
Write down in simple terms the various duties you had in a given job, like this:

FENWAY PROJECT ADMINISTRATIVE OFFICE	Boston, MA
Office Assistant	April 1999-Present

- ◆ Schedule and organize events
- ◆ Perform research and administrative tasks
- ◆ Recruit and train student interns

Step 3
Add details describing the nature of the employer in question and the purpose of the job:

FENWAY PROJECT ADMINISTRATIVE OFFICE   Boston, MA
Office Assistant   April 1999-Present
- ◆ Schedule and organize events and <u>community services for needy socioeconomic groups in inner-city Boston.</u>
- ◆ Perform research on <u>corporate and non-profit organizations to identify strategic methods for getting donations of resources.</u>
- ◆ Recruit and <u>motivate college students to participate in volunteer services.</u>

Step 4
Add quantitative details and professional terms when possible to bring the experience to life:

FENWAY PROJECT ADMINISTRATIVE OFFICE   Boston, MA
Office Assistant   April 1999-Present
- ◆ <u>In a timely manner</u>, schedule and organize events and community services <u>for over 50 inner-city Boston teenagers</u> in needy socioeconomic groups.
- ◆ Research <u>roughly 250</u> corporate and non-profit organizations to identify strategic methods for <u>soliciting</u> donations of resources.
- ◆ <u>Successfully</u> recruited and motivated <u>ten</u> college students to participate in volunteer services.

From this job description, we get a much better sense of who this student really is. We get a sense of her research experience, altruistic motives, and ability to juggle tasks—without directly mentioning these soft skills. A hiring employer could infer that the student was responsible and motivated. As you will see when you read the chapter on interviewing, these qualities are probably the most important that any potential supervisor wants to see in a new hire.

Passive versus Active Verbs
If, after all this, your resume is still lacking something, try to review your use of verbs. Remember: never use passive verbs where you can use active verbs instead. The following is a list of POWER words for inclusion in your resume.

PASSIVE VERBS	ACTIVE/POWER VERBS
Maintained	Enhanced
Assisted	Contributed (to)
Answered	Directed
Spoke to...	Resolved problems
Sold	Increased sales by...
Taught	Instructed
Processed	Expedited
Received	Earned
Coordinated	Negotiated

As mentioned earlier, a more comprehensive list of action verbs in various categories is available toward the back of this chapter.

COMPUTER SKILLS (or SPECIAL SKILLS)

This is a very important section and should be included on your resume. Every college student will have at least some basic computer skills. This is the place to state what they are. Do not overstate your abilities, but don't be modest either. You need to state your abilities clearly. Are you proficient with, familiar with, or do you just have exposure to a particular software program? Can you work with IBM PCs, Macintosh or both? In this technological age, stating your computer skills can be the edge you need to get an interview—even when pursuing jobs in supposedly non-technical fields such as the humanities and social sciences!

With this in mind, let's take a closer look at how to capture your computer skills on this section of a resume. Sometimes people either will forget about what PC skills they have or—incredibly—feel that they can't put a given skill down because they learned it on their own, outside of the classroom or workplace. Did you know that some employers are actually *more* impressed with candidates who taught themselves how to use software applications? Even if you taught yourself "just for fun," that says a great deal about your ability and enthusiasm to learn on the computer. With this in mind, here's a quick checklist you can use to determine whether you have included *all* of your relevant computer application experience.

Do you have experience with:

- **Word processing** (Microsoft Word, WordPerfect, etc.)

- **Spreadsheets** (Microsoft Excel, Lotus 1-2-3)

- **Databases** (Microsoft Access, dBase, Oracle, SAP, Lotus Notes, etc.)

- **Operating systems** (DOS, Windows 95/NT/2000/XP, UNIX, MacOS, etc.)

- **Programming languages** (C, C++, Pascal, Visual Basic)

- **Network administration** (Novell NetWare, Windows NT, TCP/IP, etc.)

- **Internet** (HTML, FrontPage, DreamWeaver, Java, ASP, Perl, etc.)

- **Presentation graphics** (PowerPoint, Harvard Graphics)

- **Desktop publishing/graphic design** (PageMaker, Corel Draw, Adobe PhotoShop, etc.)

Many students are unsure about whether their skills with a given application are good enough to put on their resumes. Obviously, you want to be honest, but you also want to give yourself credit for what you do know. One suggestion for dealing with this dilemma is to break down your knowledge of applications under the categories of "Proficient with," "Familiar with," and "Exposure to." If you have tons of experiences with Excel, say that you proficient with it. If you know how to do formulas, alter columns and rows, and create charts and graphs but not much more, you might say that you are familiar with it. While if you have only used it a few times or your experience is in the distant past, play it safe and say that you just have exposure to Excel. This way you can be honest without selling yourself short.

You also should take care to ensure that you correctly spell the names of any computer applications that you list under the heading of "Computer Skills" or "Special Skills." Use the following list as a quick reference when proofreading your resume. Although this is particularly important if you are applying for an MIS job, everyone should try to make their resume as perfectly accurate as possible... never an easy task when it comes to the bizarre spellings of many software applications.

Correct spellings of typical MIS terms (and acceptable alternatives)	
WordPerfect	Microsoft Word (MS-Word, Word)
Microsoft Excel (MS-Excel, Excel)	Microsoft Access (MS-Access, Access)
Microsoft PowerPoint (PowerPoint)	MS-DOS (DOS)
MacOS	FoxPro
Quattro Pro	Lotus 1-2-3
Lotus Notes	HTML
Windows 3.1	Windows 95
Windows 2000	UNIX
C++	Novell NetWare
PageMaker	AutoCAD

Note that it's also acceptable—and even preferable, when possible—to include what version of a program you have worked with (i.e., Word 6.0, Novell NetWare 3.x, etc.). This is especially true with operating systems such as Windows, as there is a big difference between, say, Windows 3.1 and Windows XP.

Also note that some job descriptions may list Microsoft Office as an important part of a job. For those who don't know, Microsoft Office is actually a family of Microsoft applications (Word, Excel, Access, PowerPoint, and Mail) that some employers may buy as one complete package. If you have experience with Microsoft Office, though, we still suggest writing out all of the applications, as some employers may not be familiar with the term. Also, there are different versions of Office, so it may not be clear from that term if you know Access, for example, as that is not included in all versions of Office.

Now that you know how to capture your computer skills, let's consider other skills that you want to make sure to mention. In addition, you should include skills you have in the following areas:

- Language Skills: Fluent in..., Conversational ability in..., etc.)

- Laboratory Skills (see sidebar box)

- Licenses and Training (Real Estate, CPR, First Aid)

Capturing Skills On Your Resume – An Arts and Sciences Co-op Perspective
by Ronnie Porter

I really started noticing a few years back that students who did not have much experience and who were not explicit about their skills were not getting jobs. There may be technical skills that they've not really thought about it because they haven't practiced them on a job, but they've learned them in a laboratory setting. So I created a skills list with a set of things that they might have learned in lab that they could replicate in a work setting. I had them start communicating that to employers, and it made a huge difference. On their resume, they would have a section called Laboratory Skills. I found that that made a big difference in being successful. Employers weren't making the leap from Bio I and Bio II to the skill sets, so students had to break it out for them. The interviewer might be an HR person who might not be able to communicate effectively to the supervisor what the candidate is capable of doing.

*Ronnie Porter is the cooperative education faculty coordinator
in Biology at Northeastern University.*

Here's an example of what your skills section might look like:

SKILLS
Proficient with Lotus 1-2-3, Microsoft Word, Excel, and Netscape
Familiar with Windows 95/2000, PowerPoint, and Access
Exposure to HTML and FrontPage.
Conversational in Spanish

If you have a very strong background in computers—meaning that your knowledge goes well beyond applications such as Microsoft Office—the recent industry standard is to break out your computer skills by category. This is fairly standard for students in MIS, Computer Science, Computer Engineering, and similar majors. Here's an example:

COMPUTER SKILLS

Operating Systems:	DOS, Windows 95/98/2000, MacOS
Languages:	Visual Basic, HTML
Networking:	Windows NT, Novell NetWare 3.x, TCP/IP
Internetworking:	Netscape, Internet Explorer
Applications:	Microsoft Word 6.0, Excel, Access, PowerPoint, Lotus 1-2-3, Adobe PhotoShop, Quicken, Minitab
Exposure to:	C++, SQL, Peachtree Accounting

INTERESTS

How you spend your free time reveals another dimension of your personality, as well as important skills such as communication skills, leadership, motivation and initiative, time management, resourcefulness, organization and energy. It is a chance to include activities, hobbies and interests—to show you're well-rounded. Interests humanize you—and anything that makes you seem more like a real person than just a name on a page will make an employer more inclined to give you an interview.

Resumes – An Employer's Perspective
by Mike Naclerio
An "Interests" section is a good icebreaker for interviews. It gives the resume a personal/unique touch and is an area I always seek out to open conversations with students in an interview.
   Mike Naclerio is the Director of Relationship Management at the workplace HELPLINE.

As before, try to be specific: Listing "dancing, reading, sports, and movies" is much less interesting than, say, "ballet, contemporary short fiction, ice hockey, and foreign films." A specific and unique list is much more likely to catch the eye of a potential employer. It also shows that you are serious about your interests and have some depth of character. This makes you come off as a three-dimensional person, and it also can make an employer want to get to know you a little better in the interview. As an ice-breaker question, interviewers may ask you about one of your interests... which is a MUCH easier first question than, say, "Why should we hire you for this job?" Better still, a potential employer may share one of your interests and believe (rightly or wrongly) that the two of you share a connection as a result. That can't hurt!

If you include political or religious organizations or affiliations, be aware that this could work for you or against you. Choosing not to hire you for these reasons would be illegal, of course, but you still run a risk in including certain kinds of information. Imagine writing about your volunteer work for the Republican Party on your resume, then going into your interviewer's office and seeing an autographed photo of former President Clinton! In other words, try to be sensitive to the fact that others may not share your enthusiasms and may even be turned off by them.

Avoid anything that might be controversial or that may raise a potential concern. This includes such common college student interests as nightclubs, partying, heavy metal, hanging out with friends, or shopping. You want to show interests that require some intelligence or at least energy.

As a part of your resume, some consider the Interests section to be optional or irrelevant. However, make every effort to include it. It can't hurt you, and it might help you. If you don't think you have the space, take a close look at the rest of the resume and ask yourself why you can't *make* room for this section. If I have students who are skeptical about including this section, I always ask them: "What would you prefer as the first question of your interview: "Why should we hire YOU for this job?" or "I noticed that you're interested in contemporary fiction. Who are your favorite authors?"

Here is a sample Interests section:

INTERESTS
Russian literature, skiing, chess, current events, triathlons, and camping

---

REFERENCES

And, lastly, don't forget your references and reference page. On your resume, simply write either "References Furnished Upon Request" or "References Available Upon Request" on the bottom. But don't stop there. Create a reference page on the same bond paper that you use for your resume.

Be sure to contact your references first to ask their permission to be used as a reference. This will help your reference person to be more prepared and thus able to give you a better reference when called upon by an employer.

Try to include two or three professional/work references, one or two academic references and one or two character references. A character reference is a coach, a religious leader, a family friend who has known you since you were more or less in diapers, while a work reference is usually a direct supervisor.

Include name, title, company, company address, telephone number, and, if you know it, an e-mail address. As long as you include these items, the format isn't critical: some people center their references on the page, while others have them flush left. *Just make sure that whatever format you use is consistent with your resume.*

You should always bring a few copies of your reference page to an interview, so you can give them to the interviewer immediately, if asked. If you're asked to supply references, you don't want to reply "Um, uh.... Can I get it to you in a few days?" A sample of a basic but good reference page is included at the end of this chapter following the sample resumes.

SAMPLE RESUMES

At the end of this chapter, we have included a few sample resumes that you can review to see how other students have captured themselves on resumes. These resumes reflect varying degrees of education and job experience as well as many different business majors, but they all have something unique and effective about them.

Look at Lana Schillman's resume on page 55. This is an example of the bulleted list form of resume, as opposed to the paragraphing format. One nice thing about this resume is that she has used the font Arial. As mentioned earlier, employers see many resumes in Times New Roman, which looks fine but doesn't stand out. Elsewhere, this resume has consistent and strong verbs throughout the job descriptions, and it is easy to read.

Of course, this is the resume of a senior: the kind of resume that we hope you have when you're looking for one last co-op job. But what if you're looking for your *first* co-op job? Consider the next resume at the end of this chapter. Ian Barren uses a simple but effective approach. He uses the bullet format, which works nicely. Bullets tend to work well in jobs involving a variety of duties and/or jobs that are relatively uncomplicated. This student does use transferable skills effectively, but he opted against in-depth job descriptions. I think this is probably wise. Some jobs are so basic that it is best not to try to make them seem more than they are. The jobs listed here are manual labor jobs. We could dress up the job descriptions with fancy language, having Ian call himself a "sanitation maintenance specialist" instead of a floor cleaner, but sometimes that works against you: It may seem like you're using a smokescreen of language and/or bending the truth a little too much. A safer approach is to add transferable skills and describe the actual work as clearly as you can. You shouldn't feel ashamed to put a job on your resume just because it was not glamorous or in an office environment.

The third sample resume is a great example for international students. Look how much background information LaGuardia Community College student Eva Mendez has been able to pack on one page, all without overcrowding. By conserving space with her heading, she has managed to explain a great deal about her educational history, including relevant courses. She breaks out two different jobs with the same employer effectively. This resume will save her considerable time when it comes to the interview. While some students with international backgrounds are compelled to explain their personal history in the interview, Eva should be able to move right into why the employer should hire her. After all, they already know a good deal about who she is before she even walks in the door.

Next we have another promising student from LaGuardia Community College. Like the first individual we sampled, here is a student whose job experience is longer and stronger than that of many college students. As a result, Pui Sze opts against using the transferable skills within the job description: Her experience

44

doesn't need as much selling as someone who has never had a professional job. She cuts to the point quickly, laying out what she's done on her jobs. Appropriately, she chooses to push her computer skills higher up on the resume, just after the education section. This is her top selling point, and she wants it to be noticed right away. The skills section breaks out her computer skills in a way that will be useful to her prospective employers: It's easy to follow both aesthetically and conceptually. Lastly, the resume is in a font called Verdana—always a good idea for an aspiring computer professional to show that she can get beyond the default fond in Word!

As for the fifth and last sample, the first thing that catches your eye with Meghan Brooke's resume is that it is neat and eye-pleasing, with nice use of boldface and italics. She has opted for a different font called Bell MT, which is a nice change from the usual Times New Roman rut. As her job experience features much less work related to her concentration, she has chosen to use transferable skills throughout all of her job descriptions in order to highlight skills that an MIS employer might want to see. Meghan chose the paragraphing format, too, probably because it saves a little space, but she could have used bullets just as easily. This resume attracted multiple interviews and a great entry-level co-op job for her.

As you can see, each of these three resumes differs significantly in terms of how to use font, boldface type, italics, centering, headings, and underlining. Some of the resume writers' choices may appeal to you more than others. There really is a great deal of flexibility in how you make your resume look, as long as you capture each of the required sections on a one-page resume, and as long as your resume is completely free of spelling mistakes or typographical errors.

Is it easy to write an effective resume? Not necessarily. As you hopefully know by now, you may have to be creative to show how some of your past job experience relates to the jobs you plan to pursue. But with considerable effort and a little assistance from your co-op coordinator and/or Career Services, you can write a resume that will help get you in the door for an interview.

MULTIPLE RESUMES

What if you are applying for jobs in more than one concentration? Perhaps you plan to apply for both finance jobs and MIS jobs, for example. One option for those who are more ambitious is to create TWO resumes: one emphasizing your desire to get a finance job, and another focusing on your strong interest and aptitude in MIS.

Is it "okay" to do this? Of course it is! In fact, trying to capture both of these interests in one resume is extremely difficult; you run the risk of coming across as someone who lacks focus or who is "jack of all trades, master of none." This should give you some incentive to consider writing more than one resume. One cautionary note, however: *It is crucial that YOU keep track of which resume has been faxed or e-mailed to each employer. If the same employer receives one of your resumes from your coordinator and another when you arrive for an interview, this will definitely work against you! This is especially true given that many coordinators now use a computerized system for e-mailing resumes—make sure to discuss using multiple resumes with your coordinator before trying to do this.*

Much of the information on each of your resumes will be identical: Obviously, this won't affect your Education section much, and you still list your places of employment. But how you describe your job experience could vary quite a bit. On a finance resume, you would emphasize work experience that relates to financial experience: budgeting, calculating, analyzing, assessing, etc. On an MIS resume, though, you might describe the same job in terms of what computer skills were required to perform these financial duties. Or, if some of your previous job related to computers but some of it didn't, then move your computer-related duties to the *top* of the job description for the MIS resume. On the finance resume, put the computer-related duties lower and don't emphasize them as strongly in your description. In your skills section, the MIS resume should be more all-inclusive, featuring the version number of each software application if possible. Even your interests might be reflected differently on each resume: You might take "investments" off of your MIS resume and add interests pertaining to learning new computer applications, Web design, foreign languages, and the Internet: all of which may be perceived more favorably by an MIS employer. Keep in mind that we're not suggesting that you *lie* about your interests and your job experiences. Just remember to emphasize those things which will be relevant to an employer in that field.

THINGS TO AVOID: OBJECTIVES AND TEMPLATES

Now that you are almost through with this chapter, you may be wondering why you have not read about starting off your resume with an objective—especially when many word-processing resume templates prompt you to include one.

First off, *don't use a word-processing template*! They may appeal to those who are lazy and/or fear that they don't know enough about word processing to make the format look good. Believe me, templates are not the answer. Templates make it extremely difficult for you to revise and update a resume, and they may force you into including or emphasizing items that are not appropriate for an aspiring co-op, intern, or senior seeking his or her first full-time job. A few times a year, someone shows me a resume that was thrown together in a few minutes using the resume template in Microsoft Word. The typical Word resume template is not that attractive—the student's address is small and hard to read, and the experience section's format is rather odd in its emphasis. We have plenty of options here that will work better for you.

As for objectives, they occasionally can be useful but usually are problematic or unhelpful. The problem is that they tend to say too much or not enough. Think about it: if you write that your objective is "To find a cost-accounting position with a growing financial services firm," then what happens if you want to or need to apply for something even slightly different? In other words, you end up pigeonholing yourself. The flip side is the objective that really doesn't say anything that we don't already know: "To find a cooperative education position that will help me grow as an aspiring health care professional." Well, I hope so!

The only exception to this rule might be if your true objective is to find something that is very different from what one might infer from your previous experience. Someone who has worked in marketing but now wants to pursue a career in early childhood education could make this crystal-clear with a good objective. Generally, though, you should avoid bothering with an objective on your resume.

After you have written your resume use the following checklist to make sure your resume meets the successful resume standard.

RESUME CHECKLIST

☐   The resume is one page in length.

☐   The resume has been carefully checked for spelling and punctuation errors as well as double-checked to make sure that all addresses and phone numbers are current.

☐   Job descriptions are grammatically correct.

☐   There are no personal pronouns (I/me).

☐   Job descriptions do <u>not</u> begin with: Responsibilities included...or Duties consisted of...

☐   Abbreviations of states are correct (i.e., MA not MA. or Mass.)

☐   The format is neat and attractive to the eye.

☐   The format is easily readable.

☐   All major components of a resume are included.

☐   Job titles are listed for each job description.

☐   Dates and place of employment are included for each work experience, and they are written in the same format each time.

☐   Telephone number(s) is(are) correct. (A common error because students tend to move frequently.)

☐   Resume will be copied on 8 1/2 X 11 inch bond paper in white or some other neutral color. Note that plain white paper should be used on resumes given to your coordinator: Nice paper sometimes looks awful when run through a fax machine!

YOUR RESUME IS A REFLECTION AND PERSONAL STATEMENT OF YOU!

Please note that these are suggestions, not requirements. Your resume is a reflection of you, and as such, you should feel comfortable and proud of its contents. While writing your resume, you will be presenting your experience and achievements in the best way possible. However, there is no room for deceit or lies on a resume. Lying on a resume is akin to plagiarism and is not acceptable at any university or in any professional workplace. Grade point averages, dates, computer skills, and achievements must be accurate and honest. You are building a professional reputation and should strive for a reputation known for its integrity.

Resumes – An Employer's Perspective
by Steve Sim

What impresses me on a resume? First of all, Honesty impresses me. If you haven't done a whole lot of HTML development work, and you put that down as a skill set, be sure you can answer specific questions about HTML.

Second, Clarity impresses me. If you are clear enough on a resume where someone who doesn't know anything about you (or potentially even positions you're interested in) can read your resume and say you're qualified, then it's going to get to my desk.

Third, Effective Use of Space impresses me. Fonts and margins can change to fit your info. One should feel comfortable using them freely.

Steve Sim is a Technical Recruiter at the Microsoft Corporation.

While writing your resume, feel free to consult with friends, advisors, teachers, employers and others whose opinions you respect. However, bear in mind that this guidebook and your co-op/internship or career services coordinator should be your number one resources. Again, be wary of your cousin's boyfriend who claims to be good at writing resumes—a person outside of your co-op program generally has no experience working with co-op students and employers and therefore may be not be a credible source of assistance. That said, *do* have several people proofread for grammatical and spelling errors. "I have employers that will teach you many things that you don't know," says Bob Tillman, co-op faculty coordinator for the civil engineering program at Northeastern University. "So on your resume, I have other concerns: let's get rid of all of the dumb mistakes." Many employers will discard your resume as soon as a typo is discovered, the theory being that if you cannot take the time to submit an error-free resume which should reflect your best effort, then the quality of your work may reflect the same low standards.

So invest your time wisely and do a superb job! There is no exact formula for a perfect resume, but rather suggestions based on experience, employer recommendations and research. Learn to do your resume well now, and you will find that this skill will be helpful to you throughout your career.

GOOD LUCK!

ACTION VERB LIST

COMMUNICATIONS

acted as liaison	demonstrated	lectured	publicized
advised	displayed	marketed	published
advocated	edited	mediated	recommended
authored	guided	moderated	referred
commented	informed	negotiated	sold
consulted	instructed	notified	trained
corresponded	interpreted	presented	translated

ADMINISTRATION

administered	distributed	managed	recruited
appointed	eliminated	motivated	referred
arranged	executed	obtained	represented
completed	governed	opened	reviewed
controlled	implemented	organized	selected
coordinated	instituted	overhauled	supervised
delegated	issued	presided	supplied
directed	launched	provided	terminated

PLANNING & DEVELOPMENT

broadened	devised	improved	prepared
created	discovered	invented	produced
designed	drafted	modified	proposed
developed	estimated	planned	

ANALYSIS

amplified	detected	forecasted	researched
analyzed	diagnosed	formulated	solved
calculated	disapproved	identified	studied
compiled	evaluated	investigated	systematized
computed	examined	programmed	tested

FINANCIAL/RECORDS MANAGEMENT

allocated	collected	logged	purchased
audited	documented	maximized	recorded
balanced	expedited	minimized	scheduled
catalogued	invested	monitored	traced
classified	inventoried	processed	updated

MANUAL LABOR

assembled	installed	operated	replaced
constructed	maintained	repaired	rewired

GENERAL TERMS

accomplished	delivered	originated	serviced
achieved	expanded	performed	strengthened
assisted	handled	provided	transformed
completed	increased	served	utilized

TRANSFERABLE SKILLS IN BUSINESS CONCENTRATIONS

MIS/Computer Science
Ability to learn quickly
Positive attitude/strong work ethic
Interpersonal skills
Computer skills (be specific)
Communication skills
Dependability/reliability
Customer-service skills
Willingness to do whatever asked
Patience
Organizational skills
Good judgment
Attention to detail
Ability to juggle multiple duties

Accounting/Finance
Positive attitude/strong work ethic
Quantitative skills
Responsibility
Computer skills (be specific)
Dependability/reliability
Organizational skills
Communication skills
Ability to learn quickly
Interpersonal skills
Ability to juggle multiple duties
Willingness to do whatever asked
Attention to detail
Ability to work in teams

Marketing
Verbal communication skills
Writing skills
Positive attitude/strong work ethic
Ability to do research
Persistence/Drive
Results-oriented personality
Customer-service skills
Selling skills/ Persuasiveness
Interpersonal skills
Computer skills (be specific)
Organizational skills
Outgoing personality
Ability to juggle responsibilities
Willingness to do whatever asked
Attention to detail
Ability to work in teams

Entrepreneurship
Initiative/self-starter
Creativity
Ability to work independently
Willingness to take risks
Ability to identify opportunities
Openness to new ideas
Willingness to play any role
Ambitiousness
Eagerness to learn
Ability to do research
Flexibility
Enthusiasm
Commitment
Willingness to work long hours
Persistence/Drive
Ability to juggle multiple duties

TRANSFERABLE SKILLS IN OTHER MAJORS

Health Sciences/Social Sciences
Interpersonal skills
Positive attitude/strong work ethic
Sensitivity/caring
Communication skills
Judgment/responsibility
Organizational skills
Attention to detail
Willingness to do whatever asked
Ability to juggle responsibilities
Reliability/dependability
Discretion and integrity
Ability to work in teams
Eagerness to learn

Engineering/Natural Sciences
Analytical skills
Ability to lay out and solve problems
Communication skills
Computer skills (be specific)
Positive attitude/strong work ethic
Attention to detail
Ability to work independently
Ability to work in teams
Ability to prioritize
Interpersonal skills
Reliability/dependability
Laboratory skills
Willingness to do whatever asked

Humanities
Communication skills
Ability to research
Presentation skills
Analytical skills
Positive attitude/strong work ethic
Reliability/dependability
Organizational skills
Interpersonal skills
Ability to work independently
Ability to work in teams
Willingness to do whatever asked

Criminal Justice/Law
Integrity
Judgment/responsibility
Analytical skills
Attention to detail
Communication skills
Positive attitude/strong work ethic
Interpersonal skills
Reliability/dependability
Ability to work independently
Ability to work in teams

TRANSFERABLE SKILL PHRASE CHEAT SHEET

If you would like to try building transferable skill phrases into your resume, try using this formula: Pick an accurate word from each column below in order to figure out how to graft a transferable skill phrase onto a bullet point or sentence in your Experience section.

Verb	Adjective	Transferable Skill	Linking Word
Demonstrated	effective	ability to learn quickly	when
Displayed	excellent	communication skills	while
Showed	outstanding	interpersonal skills	
Exhibited	strong	attention to detail	
Proved to have	solid	dependability	
Utilized	very good	attitude	
Exercised	consistent	organizational skills	
Used	exceptional	patience	
Possessed	positive	customer-service orientation	
		willingness to do whatever asked	
		ability to work in a team	
		ability to work independently	
		initiative	

Step 1: *Capture what you did in simple, straightforward way:*

♦ Cleaned out stalls at a horse farm.

Step 2: *Add quantifiable and quantitative details to make the job come alive:*

♦ Working in a busy, family-oriented horse farm, cleaned out 23 horse stalls daily.

Step 3: *If you were GOOD at the job, identify the transferable skills you used in the job and use them to create a phrase using the above formula:*

♦ Working in a busy, family-oriented horse farm, demonstrated positive attitude and willingness to do whatever asked while cleaning out 23 horse stalls daily.

You don't need a transferable skill phrase with every single sentence or bullet, but students without any directly relevant job experience probably should make sure to use at least two per job.... Assuming you were GOOD at that job! One way or another, find ways to make your resume do more than list WHAT you did... capture HOW you did it and WHY you did it well.

Lana Schillman
99 Tovar Road, Apt #6.   Chestnut Hill, MA 02167
(617) 490-9999   e-mail: lanas@aol.com

EDUCATION

NORTHEASTERN UNIVERSITY   Boston, MA
Candidate for Bachelor of Science Degree in Business Administration   May 2004
Concentration: Management Information Systems
Honors: Dean's List   **GPA:** 3.73

EXPERIENCE

ROCOCO INVESTMENTS   Boston, MA
Retail Information Services Department   June 1999 –Present
Architecture Assistant

- As a member of the system architecture group, take part in the design and development of a database application system.   Repository will be internally used as a decision support component required for impact analyses.
- Understand the systems, their interfaces, the databases and the overall architecture of the information system.
- Understand the logical model and model representation of the repository.
- Formulate the application's business requirements.
- Design and develop the application user interface utilizing PowerBuilder 5.0.

INTEGRITY FINANCIAL SERVICES   Boston, MA
Retail Financial Systems Department   June 1998 –April 1999
Systems Specialist

- As a Member of LAN restructuring task force, effectively worked toward simplifying file naming conventions on network, and combining drives.
- Created queries and reports for management evaluation, utilizing Crystal Reports.
- Created and updated Excel spreadsheets for Actuarial purposes.

HYANNISPORT CRANBERRIES INC.   Lakeville, MA
Human Resource Department, Intern   Jan. 1997 –May 1998

- Modified organization charts by utilizing Lotus Freelance Graphics software application.
- Performed queries to determine if there were suitable internal or external candidates for specific job requisitions.
- Used Resumix database to ensure that resumes are on the computer system.

SKILLS AND INTERESTS

Computer Skills: Knowledgeable in MS Access 2.0, MS Excel 5.0, MS Word 6.0, PowerBuilder 5.0, Lotus Freelance Graphics 2.0, Crystal Reports 5.0, Windows 3.1, Windows 95, Windows NT 4.0, UNIX, Mac. Familiar with C++, SQL, and Visual Basic.
Languages: Conversational in Hebrew; Exposure to Spanish.
Interests: Aerobics, cross-country skiing, contemporary fiction, and Web page design.

References furnished upon request

Ian Travis Barren
Barren.l@neu.edu

Current Address
22 Lakeheart Street
Fairfield, CT 06001
(617) 333-3333

Permanent Address
187 Fancart Drive
Dover, MA 02777
(508) 345-6789

EDUCATION

Boynton Community College   Westport, CT
Candidate for Bachelor of Science Degree in Biology
Minor: Human Services
Expected Date of Graduation: May 2007

EXPERIENCE

Bacher Nurseries Incorporated   Wilmington, MA
Stock Boy and Cashier   May 1999-June 2002
- Effectively juggled multiple tasks at times when the store was extremely busy, ringing up purchases, checking on inventory, answering the phone, and processing returns.
- Working at a small retail business selling flowers, trees, and landscaping supplies, developed good customer-service skills when associating with customers.
- Showed excellent interpersonal skills when dealing with a great variety of customers.

Shea Griffin Transportation   Boston, MA
Mover   August 1998-May 1999
- Demonstrated strong work ethic when assisting other people moving items.
- Utilized good interpersonal skills when taking orders from staff and faculty.

Munze School District   Wilmington, MA
Cleaner   June 1998-May 1999
- Performed a variety of jobs in groups, demonstrating ability to work in teams when cleaning floors, desks, walls, and tables.

COMPUTER SKILLS

Knowledgeable in Microsoft Word, Microsoft Excel, and Netscape.
Currently learning Microsoft Access and PowerPoint.

INTERESTS

Interests include Tae Kwon Do, marine animals, and lacrosse.

References will be furnished upon request.

Eva Mendez

11 23rd Place, Apt. 3D   Sunnyside, NY 11012
646-555-3333   e-mail: evamendez84@hotmail.com

Education

LaGuardia Community College/CUNY -   Long Island City, NY
September 2002 –Present

<u>Major: Education: The Bilingual Child</u> - GPA 3.91 –Phi Theta Kappa Honor Society
Completed 48 credits toward an Associate of Arts degree
<u>Relevant Coursework</u>

Introduction to Bilingualism	Early Concepts of Math for Children
General Psychology	Sociology of Education
Advanced Spanish Composition	Children's Literature

LaGuardia Community College/CUNY   Long Island City, NY
English as a Second Language –Level 6   September 2000 –May 2002

Universidad Central del Columbia   Bogota, Columbia
September 1990 –September 1994
B.A., Communications with a specialization in Public Relations

Experience

LaGuardia Community College   Long Island City, NY
English Language Center   August 2002 –June 2003
<u>Lab Assistant</u>
- Familiarized ESL faculty and students in the use of the language lab's computerized listening/recording equipment.
- Conducted student orientations to the language lab and participated in special teaching and learning projects.
- Supervised open lab hours for students' independent study.

<u>Office Assistant</u>   September 2001 –June 2002
- Assisted the Center in helping students from Latin America adjust to living and studying in the United States
- Guided students with information related to TELC programs and international student regulations

Banco Popular del Columbia   Bogota, Columbia
<u>Consumer Banker/Financial Consultant</u>   June 1998 –May 2000
- Performed administrative and financial tasks for the Human Resources Director
- Managed various financial business, including opening new accounts and providing information on loans and investments
- Prepared banking instruments and completed monetary transactions for corporate and personal clients

Skills and Interests

Proficient in MS-Word, Adobe Photoshop, QuarkExpress and Netscape. Familiar with MS-PowerPoint and Excel.
Strong marketing and organizational skills.
Fluent in Spanish; Proficient in Portuguese.
Interests: Latina writers, performing arts, black and white photography, basketball.

References Furnished Upon Request

Pui Sze Ng

57 Durutti Avenue, Staten Island, New York 10201
Phone 718-222-0000, Fax 718-222-9990, e-mail: puisze@yahoo.com

Education
LaGuardia Community College/CUNY, Long Island City, NY
Associate of Applied Science Degree – January 2001
Programming and Systems Major, Business Minor
Dean's List

Skills

Software	Programming Languages	Operating Systems
• MS Word 97/00	• Visual Basic 6.0	• Windows 9.x/NT/00
• Excel 97/00	• Visual FoxPro 6.0	• Dos 5.x/6.x
• FrontPage 97/00	• C++	• Novell Netware 4.x/5.x
• Adobe Photoshop	• HTML	• Macintosh OS 8.5

- o Customizing computers, constructing PC systems, troubleshooting and implementing software applications
- o Strong analytical skills
- o Detail-oriented and dedicated to problem-solving
- o Excellent interpersonal and organization skills

Work Experience
Manhattan University   New York, NY
Network Technician and End-User Support Specialist   August 1999 – June 2000
- Work with relative independence to meet CIS project deadlines, including the setup of computers and printers for the registration department, faculty and student labs.
- Install and configure Windows Workstations, TCP/IP, and applications.
- Run RJ-45 CAT 5 wires and terminate into Keystone jack preparing workstations for LAN services and internetworking.
- Use a variety of equipment, such as wire scope and port scanner, and applications, such as IP browser, FTP and IRC software to complete projects.

Lavoie USA   Long Island City, NY
Accounting Office Assistant   June 1998 – July 1999
- Used Excel to create accounting spreadsheets.
- Posted financial entries to journal and ledger utilizing customized software.
- Organized, sorted and maintained financial records and profiles.

Interests
Technological trends via hands-on experience, online tech resources, computer technology magazines, gourmet cooking, jazz, outdoor activities.

References
Business and personal references available upon request

MEGAN C. BROOKE

e-mail: m.brooke@neu.edu

Local Address
145 Gallatin Street
Bozeman, MT 02115
(907) 465-8822

Home Address
6856 Camera Circle
Ocala, FL 22454
(255) 788-8642

EDUCATION

HANNAH UNIVERSITY   Bozeman, MT
Bachelor of Science Degree in Nursing   May 2007
Cumulative GPA: 3.6 (4.0 scale)
Honors: University Honors Program, Dean's List
Financing 80% of tuition and living expenses through cooperative education earnings and part-time job income

TIMOTHY HIGH SCHOOL   Ocala, Florida
College Preparatory Curriculum   June 2001
Honors: Who's Who Among American High School Students, National Honor Roll,
            National Honor Society
Activities: Varsity Tennis, Ocala Packers Hiking Club, Students Against Driving Drunk

EXPERIENCE

KOHL'S DEPARTMENT STORE   Ocala, Florida
Point of Sale Representative   June 2000-September 2001
Increased customer participation in Kohl's credit program by persuading customers to enroll. Exhibited close attention to detail while performing cash and credit transactions and calculating customer receipts. Demonstrated ability to learn quickly while using the credit computer and cash register. Greeted customers.

GOLDEN YEARS SENIOR CENTER   Ocala, Florida
Volunteer   June 1998-September 1999
Demonstrated warmth and caring when working with over 75 geriatric residents. Consistently exhibited patience while dealing with demanding population on a daily basis. Effectively juggled multiple duties by answering phones, delivering food, mail, and engaging in personal conversations with residents. Taught interested residents how to use Internet. Stocked supplies.

COMPUTER SKILLS

Knowledgeable in Microsoft Word, Microsoft Excel, Windows, and Netscape
Familiar with Microsoft Access, Microsoft PowerPoint, and HTML

INTERESTS

Skiing, ice hockey, camping, Norwegian literature, drawing, and theater.

References will be furnished upon request

MEGAN C. BROOKE
e-mail: m.brooke@neu.edu

<u>Local Address</u>
145 Gallatin Street
Bozeman, MT 02115
(907) 465-8822

<u>Home Address</u>
6856 Camera Circle
Ocala, FL 22454
(255) 788-8642

REFERENCES

Ms. Zofia Profizer, Store Manager
Kohl's Department Store
777 South Garfield Drive
Ocala, Florida 22454
(255) 555-3388
e-mail: zprofizer@kohls.com

Ms. Danielle DiCoscia
Golden Years Senior Center
5544 Manatee Highway
Ocala, Florida 22455
(255) 555-3000
e-mail: azamboni@goldenyears.com

Ms. Susan Bacher, Family Friend
43 Locklear Cove
Kissimmee, Florida 22103
(313) 555-1111
e-mail: krisdelmhorst@hotmail.com

Dr. Joseph Pepitone, Professor
Timothy Paul School of Nursing
Hannah University
24 Lone Mountain Avenue
Bozeman, MT 90601
(906) 373-0001
e-mail: j.pepitone@hannah.edu

Dr. Singha Piqaboue, Associate Professor
Timothy Paul School of Nursing
Hannah University
24 Lone Mountain Avenue
Bozeman, MT 90601
 (906) 373-0003
e-mail: s.piqaboue@hannah.edu

Chapter 2 Review Questions

1. Name at least four transferable skills that you have to offer a potential employer, and identify where you developed each skill.

2. Does it always make sense to list job experience in reverse chronological order, starting with the most recent job? Why, or why not?

3. What are the pros and cons of specifically listing your transferable skills on a resume?

4. What is the best way to indicate your varying degrees of knowledge of a computer skill or a language?

5. Name five specific interests that you have, choosing only ones that would add value to your resume. Also, list three interests that should NOT be included on any resume.

CHAPTER THREE
Strategic Interviewing

INTRODUCTION

When I am helping a student prepare for an interview, sometimes I am asked the following question: "Should I try to make it sound like I would be a great candidate for this job, or should I be honest?"

My answer is, simply, "Yes." Many future co-ops, interns, and full-time job seekers don't realize that this is not an either/or question: There is no reason why you can't be honest while effectively selling yourself as an outstanding job candidate. Learning to do so is a two-step process: You need to identify which of your skills, experiences, or personal characteristics might be attractive to a particular employer. Then you need to learn how to articulate these qualities to the interviewer in the process of answering questions... and asking questions!

By the end of this chapter, you should have a better idea of how to strategize for interviews: How to show the employer that there is a strong connection between your unique characteristics as a job candidate and the job itself, as it is described in the job description.

Mastering this art will boost your chances of obtaining the best jobs. Depending on our major, the job market, the interviewer's approach, and your school's way of doing business with employers, your interview could be anything from a brief "sanity check" to a grueling interrogation. Talk to the professional at your school about what to expect, but—when in doubt—always assume that the interview will be a challenging test of your ability to research, prepare, and execute strategically.

BASICS OF INTERVIEWING

Before your resume has been transmitted to a potential employer, there are several basics that you should know about interviewing. While many may seem like common sense, sometimes we find that sense is less common than we would like to believe. Accordingly, see how you rate in terms of the following:

Answering Machine/Service

Owning an answering machine—or at least lining up a call answering service—is essential during the interview process. Better yet, obtain a machine or service that you can access from a remote site. In other words, you want something that you can check whether you are at home, school, work, etc. The best employers know that they need to act quickly if they hope to hire the best co-op candidates. If they have trouble contacting you, they may move ahead and hire someone else. At the very least, they may experience frustration in attempting to contact you. Obviously, this is *not* the kind of first impression you want to make. So get a machine or service, and check it at least twice each day once you start the referrals process.

There is a definite dilemma with phone service for many students in this day and age: Some students fear putting their home number on a resume due to unreliable or obnoxious roommates. Yet if they put their cell phone number on the resume, then you run the risk of having an employer call you while you're on a noisy subway or some other awkward situation. With a wireless phone, you also have to worry about annoying delays, echoes, and garbled speech depending on the quality of your service.

There is no easy solution to this dilemma. If you really can't trust your roommates, you may want to consider using your cell phone or perhaps even the home number at the address of a parent. If you DO use a cell phone, though, be super-careful about when and where you pick up the phone when you are in the thick of a job search. If at all possible, use the cell phone to receive messages from employers—call them back on a dedicated line in a quiet environment.

Another point on this topic: Your answering machine message and initial conversation will give the potential employer their first opportunity to hear how you present yourself. As such, you want to leave a highly professional message, one that is clear, concise, and well spoken. For example: *"Hi, you've reached 555-1234. We cannot answer your call right now, but please leave a message, and we will call you back as soon as possible."* There have been many horror stories about students leaving messages with loud music, obnoxious roommates saying ridiculous things: "Hey, we're down at the pub with a bunch of pitchers—Later!" We had one student whose *girlfriend* left a rather provocative message on his machine—not the best introduction to a potential employer! Sometimes it's not even clear whether the caller has dialed the right number. On a more subtle note, many students simply mumble, sound half-asleep, or fail to express themselves in an upbeat, professional manner.

Basically, an answering machine message won't determine whether or not you get a job. At best, it may be completely neutral. At worst, it can create the beginnings of doubt about whether you have the basic professionalism to communicate in a corporate environment. And if life without a humorous answering machine message seems unbearable, you can always change your message back after you have started your co-op job.

Phone Etiquette

When speaking to a potential employer on the phone, make sure to be professional in your speech. Try to avoid "yeahs" and "uh-huhs." Speak with energy and enthusiasm—even if you're not sure if you want this particular job. You want your first conversation with a potential employer to be very positive and effective. If you're called to arrange an interview, make sure that you have your calendar on hand. Try to be flexible about what days and times you can meet. If you have another commitment, say so politely and suggest what days would be best for you. Tell the caller that you're looking forward to the interview and eager to find out whether this job would be a good match for your skills. Make sure to ask for directions to the interview, ask for the individual's phone number in case you must reschedule the interview due to an emergency, and confirm the date and time before you hang up.

Attire

Make sure that your professional wardrobe is in good shape *before* beginning the interview process. Many students have wound up buying a new suit or outfit right before going on an interview: In fact, one student forgot to take the price and size tags off of his new suit and was nicknamed "Tags" for his whole six-month co-op job! You don't want to be shopping before an interview when you could be researching the organization, so plan ahead.

Men should wear dress shoes, a suit, a shirt, and tie. Your shoes should be polished. Your suit preferably should be some shade of gray, blue, or black... NOT some unusual color like green, flamingo pink, etc. Go light on cologne. As for ties, it is generally best to be conservative: Wear something that doesn't stand out too much. To our knowledge, no one has ever failed to get a job because they wore a boring tie. This rule is especially true of jobs in conservative fields, such as finance, accounting, and criminal justice. If in doubt, check with your co-op coordinator.

Women should wear dress shoes, nylons, a dress or a skirt and blouse, or a suit. Make-up should not be excessive; wear little or no perfume as well. If you're applying for finance and accounting jobs, a very conservative suit would be appropriate. Although some women balk at wearing nylons—and there are co-op jobs where they may not be considered necessary—you should always wear them for interviews... even on hot summer days.

Some students object to these guidelines, feeling that their individuality is being compromised. Well, that's true. Basically, if having a pierced tongue or nose ring, a mohawk haircut or other alternative hairstyle, or wearing funky clothes is more important to you than getting a job, go right ahead but be prepared to accept the consequences. Fairly, or unfairly, potential employers *will* judge you based on how you present yourself at an interview. Are you really interested in "fitting in" and "being one of the team," or is it more important to make a statement about your individuality with your appearance? The choice is yours.

Hygiene

You shouldn't have to receive a gift-wrapped bar of soap from a friend, roommate, or co-op coordinator to know that hygiene is an important consideration. In an interview, hygiene is either neutral or a negative; it goes unnoticed or it distracts the interviewer from the task at hand.

You should shower or bathe before any interview. Make sure your hair is neat and clean. Use deodorant, and make a habit of having a breath mint on the way to an interview. It can be a real distraction, and no one wants to work next to someone who has a hygiene problem!

Punctuality

Short of death—your own or that of an immediate family member—or hospitalization, there is never really an acceptable reason to be late for an interview or to fail to show up altogether. Even arriving with a few minutes to spare can only increase any anxiety you feel about being interviewed. With this in mind, there are a few things you can do to avoid being late to interviews:

- Set your watch ten minutes ahead.

- Go to the office the day before to make sure that you can find it, and so you know how long it takes to get there. Frequently, the interviewer will meet you in the lobby and ask you if you had trouble finding the office. Imagine what he or she will think of you if you respond by saying, "Oh, no... I drove out here yesterday to make sure that I could find the building, so I had no trouble being on time today." This is far preferable to beginning the interview with some excuse about why you're ten minutes late.

- Assume that the trip will take you 30 minutes longer than you expect it will. If you allow a great deal of extra time, the worst-case scenario is that you will arrive 30 to 60 minutes early. If you do arrive early, you could use the extra time to review the job description, review your research, and go over questions you would like to ask the interviewer. If you're completely prepared, take a brisk walk around the block to put any excess nervous energy to use. Don't go into the reception area an hour early—that can be awkward for the interviewer, who may feel obliged to see you sooner than the scheduled time. At most, arriving 20-30 minutes early is reasonable.

PREPARING FOR A SPECIFIC INTERVIEW

Working with a co-op/internship coordinator or career services professional, you will look at job descriptions and choose several jobs that you wish to target. So what do you do after an employer calls you and arranges an interview? For any employer, be sure to bring extra copies of your resume and the names, addresses, and phone numbers of your references on nice paper. But how do you prepare for an interview for one *specific* employer? Let's consider several steps in the preparation process:

Knowing the job description

First, make sure that you have a copy of the job description. Take it home with you, and memorize all the specific skills that the employer is looking for in a job candidate. Start thinking about how the employer would think of you as a job candidate in terms of the skills needed for the job. What would the employer perceive to be your strengths? Your weaknesses? Try to understand what it was about your resume that attracted your employer as well as what concerns you may need to overcome to get the job.

Researching the organization

Doing strong research on potential employers is one thing that separates excellent job seekers from average ones. Start by asking your co-op or career services professional. They may have student job descriptions that they can share with you; they may have visited the site. Best of all, they might be able to give you contact information for someone who has already worked in that exact position! Imagine what you could ask that person to prepare yourself. This takes a little initiative, but this step can give you eye-popping information to use in the interview: "I spoke to Debby Birkbeck about her experience as a co-op, and I was excited to hear that there are opportunities to work closely with patients at your site." You may want to ask about the size of the company, the nature of the work, the organization's culture, the possibility for employment after graduation or in future co-op periods, etc.

For general company information, your school library can be a valuable resource. Talk to a reference librarian if necessary about how to find company news. For publicly-traded companies, you can find recent news at websites such as www.nasdaq.com or at any number of financial services websites. Once you have assembled several sources, look them up and take notes on what you read. Companies will be impressed if you have done significant homework before the interview.

Here are some other tips for searching via the Web:

Learn how to use more than one search engine: The Internet contains a vast amount of information, and it's easy to get lost in the web. Try using more than one means of obtaining information to ensure that you get the best available website. Here are some useful Web addresses for doing Internet research:

www.google.com
www.altavista.com
www.dogpile.com
www.yahoo.com/Business_and_Economy/Companies/
www.excite.com

If you go into any of these sites, you generally will have to type in the name of the company, then scan through the different website summaries to find the one which is the closest match for your research purposes. Don't be fooled! Many companies have similar names or various branches in different locations: Make sure you're researching the right one.

With some of the most powerful search engines—like Alta Vista—a few little tricks will greatly enhance the effectiveness of your search. For example, don't just type in John Hancock, because it will pull up every website that has the name "John" or "Hancock" in it... which is NOT very helpful. Instead, type in a colon between the words John:Hancock. Or put quotes around the word: "John Hancock". This tells the search engine that you ONLY want sites that have that combination of words.

Leave no stone unturned in your research: In my experience, students give up far too easily when doing research for an interview. Here's an example: A small company interviewed six of my students one time. Five looked in the files, looked in the library, looked on the Internet, and found NOTHING. They gave up. The sixth student did all of the same things and also found nothing. But he kept trying. He looked at the job description again, and saw this phrase: "We provide software solutions for the vending industry." He decided to go back to the library and back onto the Internet, learning as much as he could about the vending industry and how software was utilized in it. He learned a LOT about the industry, the competition, and key issues that probably were facing his potential employer. Then he walked around campus with a notebook, looking at the vending machines: Who made them? Who serviced them? How sophisticated were they in terms of software? Armed with this information, he was able to have a sophisticated conversation with the interviewer about vending. And, of course, he got the job. So remember, you can use the Internet to research the *industry* and the *competition* as well as the company itself.

In similar ways, you need to think creatively about your research: If the product/service is consumer-oriented, go see it in action or how it is displayed and sold. Talk to people who might use the product or service, and ask them their opinions of it. Get a feel for the *job* as well as the company.

Another creative approach is to research terms on the job description that you don't understand. Let's say a job description mentions that you will be using a Crystal Reports database to do research on market segmentation. If you aren't familiar with that software application and/or with the concept of marketing segmentation, get on the Internet and use word searches until you come up with something. Anybody can say that they are a quick learner when they are being interviewed, but few people *demonstrate* their ability to learn quickly by doing appropriate research for an interview. Obviously, you can't learn a software application overnight, but with a little effort you can learn enough to have an intelligent conversation with the interviewer.

Strategic Interviewing – A Co-op Student's Perspective
by Ted Schneider
RESEARCH, RESEARCH, RESEARCH! It is extremely embarrassing to show an interviewer that you have not prepared by researching the company or its clients. During my Microsoft interview, the interviewer asked me to "describe an issue facing Microsoft currently - besides the unfair business practices/monopolization issue." As you may have guessed, I had nothing to say.
    Ted Schneider was an Accounting/MIS student at Northeastern University, Class of 2002.

Any information that you can dig up may prove useful in the interview. Later in this chapter, we will show specific ways that you can impress an interviewer with the fruits of your research.

STRATEGIZING

Matching Your Skills To The Employer's Needs
The most crucial aspect of a great interview is demonstrating that your skills and personal qualities are a great match for what the employer needs in a co-op worker. You may have excellent grades, terrific skills, and a great attitude, but if you can't explain why YOU are a great MATCH for THIS JOB, you may be out of luck. You need to have concrete reasons that reflect specific information on the job description. If a co-op candidate fails to strategize in this way, the employer may tell the co-op coordinator something like this: "Mary seemed like a great person with good skills, and I really liked her attitude. But I'm not convinced that she meets our needs."

How can you avoid being "close but not quite" when going after a job? Consider the following example. The Littlefield Rehabilitation Center has a nursing co-op job available for a student with "great empathy and patience, some experience working with the elderly or disabled, a basic understanding of nursing, and a willingness to work long shifts."

Student 1 and Student 2 have identical skills: Both are solid "B+" students who have only limited experience with the elderly. Both have taken only prerequisite coursework in nursing, but they do have volunteer experience working in hospitals during school vacations.

In the interview, both students are asked the following question: "Why should we hire you for this position?"

Student 1 says: "I'm a hard worker, and I've always wanted to work for an rehabilitation center. I think this job would give me a lot of good experience, especially the exposure to the geriatric population. So I look at this as a great opportunity."

Student 2 says: "I know you're looking for someone who is extremely patient and empathic. Here are my references—please call my supervisor at the hospital and ask her specifically about those qualities. As for working with the elderly, my experience is limited—but in preparing for the interview today, I talked to some students who worked at your Center; it sounds like you are doing some amazing things with treatment! Looking on the Internet, I was surprised to find that a third of your beds are utilized by younger patients recovering from head injuries, so I've already started reading up on subarachnoid hemorrhages and their clinical manifestations—I want to be ready to hit the ground running in this job! As you can see on my resume, my real strength is working with people, whether I've worked as a hospital volunteer or as a waitress. So I think I bring a strong background to this position."

Who would you be more inclined to hire? Neither student has excellent skills, but Student 2 did a much better job of showing the employer the connections between her skills and the job description. Student 1 answered the questions more in terms of why she or he would like to have the job instead of focusing on why the employer would want to hire her. As such, the employer might see this student as a far better match for the job... even though the two students have identical skills!

By tying your answers to the job description, you show the potential employer that:
- you are industrious enough to prepare effectively for an interview.

- you are persuasive, self-confident, and sensitive to the employer's needs.

- you have an awareness of what your skills are and how ready you will be to do the job well—right from the start.

One good tip is to go into any job interview with a solid strategy featuring three or four compelling reasons why the interviewer should hire you to do that specific job. Being focused like this will make a big difference.

We will consider more examples when we look more closely at interview questions.

VERBAL AND NONVERBAL INTERVIEWING SKILLS

Obviously, interviewers are very interested in what you have to say. However—especially in some fields—employers are interested in *how* you say it. Many interviewers may not consciously notice what you're doing right or wrong in this sense, but these behaviors still may have a critical impact on whether or not you get a job offer.

Verbal Skills
Keep in mind the following when interviewing.

Speak at a reasonably loud volume. Make sure the interviewer can hear and understand you. If you're not sure, ask.

Don't speak too fast. If you speak quickly, the interviewer may miss the strong points that you are making, or simply fail to remember. Slow down: especially when making an important selling point about yourself. When asked a question, don't be afraid to pause before answering or between giving each of two or three points about yourself. Don't be afraid of pauses: Brief silences can be effective in allowing points to sink in or to emphasize something strongly.

It's easy to overlook just how *hard* it is to be an interviewer: All at once, the interviewer has to listen to your answer while trying to assess your answer and think about the next question to ask. If you never come up for air or give time for your points to be digested, the interviewer won't remember much of what you've said. One interviewer told me that I "use silence effectively" as an interviewee. I thought that was a strange compliment at first—aren't interviews all about what you say? Really, though, she was just saying that I was giving her enough time to juggle all her various thoughts as an interviewer.

Watch out for "verbal tics." We all have verbal tics, y'know? Um.... you should, like, try to not use them during an interview, y'know? Yeah, they like make you seem totally immature and unprofessional, right?

Seriously: Almost everyone has a tendency to fill the empty seconds between phrases and sentences with little bits of meaningless slang. Doing this occasionally will go unnoticed, but doing it repeatedly can become a major distraction. In practice interviews, I have heard students use the word "like" as many as 12 times in one sentence! Many people don't even believe they use these phrases constantly until they see themselves on videotape. Slowing down your speech will help reduce these annoying, meaningless phrases. If you fail to reduce these phrases, you may come off as very young, inarticulate, immature, or unprepared. It takes practice to get out of these habits, but it's worth it, y'know?

Speak with a professional tone. Save your slang expressions for conversations with friends and significant others. When describing your job experience, for example, avoid terms like "stuff" and "things." Be precise; use a broader range of vocabulary.

Vary your tone. Avoid speaking in a monotone. Make your voice sound excited when talking about things that interest you. This will keep the listener interested.

If English is not your primary language: Make sure that you know how to answer typical interview questions in English. Speak loudly and slowly, and cheerfully offer to repeat something or rephrase something if the interview doesn't seem to understand you. If asked about your understanding and use of English, discuss what you have done and will do in order to improve your communication skills in English. If appropriate, you might also mention previous job experiences in which employers were concerned about your English skills but eventually found that this was not a problem for you or your co-workers.

Nonverbal skills

People can often say a great deal in an interview without even opening their mouths. Therefore, pay attention to the following guidelines:

Handshakes: Shake hands firmly when meeting the interviewer or anyone he or she introduces you to. Keep your thumb up as you extend your hand to shake. If you tend to get sweaty palms when you're nervous, try to wipe off your hand frequently (and subtly) while waiting for the interviewer to arrive in the lobby.

Eye Contact: As much as possible, make eye contact with the interviewer. Don't stare, but don't let your eyes wander around the room at any time; you may be perceived as having a short attention span or as being uninterested in the job.

Body Language: Sit up straight, and lean forward a little when being interviewed. Don't slouch, lean way back, or fold your arms: This comes off as being defensive, laid-back, or unfriendly. When you're not using your hands or arms to help express a point, keep them on your lap. Don't put them in your pockets, as you may distract the interviewer by jangling change. Avoid drumming your fingers, fiddling with your hair, pen, jewelry, or clothes, and never chew gum. Try to *smile*!

Using notes/Taking notes: There is no simple answer to this question. In some fields (i.e., marketing), job interviews are comparable to making a formal sales presentation. In this case, failing to use notes may indicate that you have done little preparation for your interview/presentation. You will give the impression that you are "winging it," which—even if you're good at it—may not send the message you want to send. Conversely, other business employers might feel that relying on notes indicates that you are *not* adequately prepared.

When moderating a co-op employer discussion panel recently, I was intrigued to hear that some employers are very impressed when an interviewee takes notes during the interview. These employers felt that the note takers were showing sincere interest and good attention to detail. They cautioned, however, that you need to be judicious in exactly what you right down. Otherwise, note-taking can be very distracting and also may keep you from making adequate eye contact.

In most cases, using notes or taking notes will not be necessary in business interviews. But if you are afraid of "blanking out" or failing to cover several points, you might try using them... as long as you are not reading directly from them or looking at them constantly. Marketing majors should be prepared to use notes more often than not. If you are unsure about what is most appropriate for your field, ask your coordinator. We will talk more about how to use notes later in this chapter.

TURNING NERVOUS ENERGY INTO AN ALLY

Some people enjoy interviews, but most people experience at least some nervousness about them. Feeling nervous is a completely normal and rational reaction to going on an interview. After all, you want to make a good impression, and you want to make sure you get the best possible job for each co-op period. You care! That's a good thing.

One big mistake that many individuals make is believing that their goal should be to eliminate any nervousness that they feel. The more you try to order yourself to be relaxed, the harder it becomes to do so.

Here is a more helpful strategy: Remember that nervousness is nothing more than energy. The last thing you want to do is go into an interview without any energy! The trick is to *use* your nervous energy in positive ways. If you begin to feel nervous during an interview, put that excess energy to use by:

- speaking louder and with more enthusiasm

- using your hands to be more expressive instead of keeping your arms folded

- focusing harder on the interviewer, listening closely to what he or she is saying

- pushing yourself to come up with excellent questions and answers

Perhaps most importantly, remember another important fact about nervousness: *People can never tell exactly how nervous you are if you don't tell them.* In mock interviews, many of my students will openly admit that they're nervous. This is a mistake. The interviewer can rarely tell if a student is nervous, and admitting nervousness sometimes makes the interviewer focus on trying to determine how nervous the person is instead of really listening to his or her answers. In some cases, admitting nervousness may make the interviewer feel awkward or nervous too. Regardless, discussing nervousness only moves you both further away from determining whether you are a good match for the job.

Interviewing – A Student's Perspective
by Mark Moccia

I fit the "sweaty palms" prototype perfectly on my first interview. I previously worked in an office environment, although I did not have a formal interview because my mother hired me! I thought I would not be as nervous because of the ease with which I handled my practice interviews. Despite my glowing confidence from the day before, I was nervous from the moment I woke up that morning. When I arrived at the office, I was sweating as if it were 100 degrees outside; the only problem with this is that it was only 75 degrees and cloudy! I experienced all the nightmares that come with nervous first interviews; I stumbled over words, dropped things on the floor, and apologized 50 times, along with many other little, embarrassing moments.

The most important lesson I learned from this interview is to relax and be yourself. I was trying too hard to impress the interviewer (who was the president of the company, which did not help matters) when I should have been selling myself more. It is important to impress the interviewer but you have to earn this right through hard work. You simply cannot impress the interviewer with your "uncanny multi-tasking ability" if you have never experienced multi-tasking.

It is important to figure out your strengths and sell those to the interviewer. It is also important to figure out your weaknesses and what you are doing to improve on them because interviewers will ask that question frequently. Finally, as mentioned earlier, the more research you perform on the company before the interview, the more questions you will have for them at the end of the interview when you hear the dreaded, "Do you have any questions for me?" This was pretty ugly for my first interview; I believe my response was, "Uh, uh, no. I do not believe I can learn anything else from this interview." BIG MISTAKE!

Mark Moccia was an Accounting/MIS student at Northeastern University, Class of 2002.

Here are a few other ideas about how to keep nervous energy from becoming a negative force for you in interviews:

- Formulate a specific strategy for each interview: Come up with at least three specific reasons why YOU should be hired for THAT specific job description.

- Prepare yourself thoroughly by considering how you would answer typical questions and by doing extensive research about the company.

- Allow yourself plenty of time to travel to the interview location.

- Practice your interviewing skills by working with your co-op/internship coordinator or with the Career Services Department.

- Practice answering questions with a friend, roommate, or family member.

People who learn to use their nervous energy effectively come off as energetic, enthusiastic, motivated, and focused in interviews... even though they have butterflies and knots in their stomach the whole time!

ORDINARY QUESTIONS, EXTRAORDINARY ANSWERS

Although it is impossible to anticipate every question that an employer will ask you in an interview, you should be prepared to answer the typical questions that arise in many interviews. Preparation makes an enormous difference in being able to deliver extraordinary answers to ordinary questions.

Individuals with little interviewing experience seldom give "bad" answers to questions. However, many people fail to understand the difference between a pretty good answer and an extraordinary one. In this section, we will dissect the most common interview questions and show you specific examples of mediocre, ordinary, and outstanding answers to these questions.

1. *"Tell me about yourself."*
In one form or another, this is a fairly common opening question. You may be asked about your background, or about what kind of person you are. Many people—particularly those who have failed to prepare—dislike these questions and struggle to answer them. The question seems incredibly broad and general: There are a thousand things you could talk about. However, those who are well prepared look forward to this kind of question. Basically, the interviewer is giving you a very open-ended question: You could choose to talk about almost anything in your response.

Why do interviewers ask this question? For one thing, it's an ice-breaker, a way of easing into the interview before asking tough questions about your skills. Another reason employers ask this is because it's a quick way to test your judgment. What you choose to say about yourself says a great deal about your personality and character.

There are many possible ways to answer this question effectively. Here are some guidelines to bear in mind:

1. *Don't waste time telling interviewers what they already know.* Many students answer this question too literally, telling the interviewer that they go to Northeastern, that they're a finance major, etc. Your resume and the fact that it was faxed by a given co-op coordinator makes this kind of response very obvious.

2. *If you're not given a specific question, focus on why YOU are a good candidate for THIS specific job.* An open-ended question is always a good opportunity to sell yourself. Talk about what the job description requires and why you represent a good match for these requirements.

3. *If you are an unconventional candidate for a job, discuss why you are interested in this job and why you are a strong candidate.* For example, if you're a finance major who is interviewing for an accounting or MIS job, you should explain why you are excited about an opportunity in one of these fields and how this job relates to your career goals. In other words, anticipate an employer's concern and deal with it enthusiastically.

Let's look at some possible answers to *"Tell me about yourself."*

Mediocre answer:	*"I live in Brookfield; I'm an accounting major; I like sports, reading, and rollerblading, and I would like to get this job with your company."*
Ordinary answer:	*"I'm a hard worker, and I've got solid grades and good co-op experience. I think this job would be really interesting, and I'm eager to learn from this experience. I'm persistent, and I expect a lot of myself."*
Extraordinary answer:	*"Working in public accounting is my objective. I have excellent grades in my accounting classes, and I did a great deal of bookkeeping in my first co-op job. I have a strong combination of classroom and professional skills, and I'm dedicated to proving myself in a public accounting environment."*

Can you see how different these responses are? The first tells the interviewer almost nothing that couldn't be inferred from reading the resume. The second conveys a positive attitude but tells the interviewer nothing about why the person would be good for THIS job as opposed to any other position. The third response shows that the job candidate read the job description carefully and has thought a great deal about why the position is a good match for his or her skills and traits. It also shows initiative by referring to research that the candidate did to prepare for the interview (provided the candidate really DID do that research). With this kind of response, you can go a long way toward showing an employer how your skills connect with a given job opportunity.

But what if the employer really was asking the question to find out more about your interests outside of work? Well, he or she can always ask a more specific follow-up question, which you can answer accordingly.

**2. "I see on your resume that you're interested in _____.
Tell me more about that."**
This is another common ice-breaker question. Some employers may ask about your interest in books or skiing or whatever in order to help you relax and have a less artificial conversation with them.

This type of question also illustrates why you should always list some of your hobbies and interests on your resume. Basically, an employer is hiring an individual: not just a list of skills and qualifications. Talking about your hobbies and interests gives you an opportunity to make yourself a real person in the employer's eyes: hopefully, a person they would enjoy working with for a lengthy period of time. Believe it or not, this type of question can also help you sell yourself for the job, sometimes in subtle ways.

For example, one of the first questions that *I* get asked in most interviews is about my interest in writing fiction. When I get asked about it, I'm delighted: For one thing, it gives me a chance to speak about something with great enthusiasm. More importantly, though, this type of question allows me to convey personal qualities that may be very useful in the job at hand. If a job requires creativity, communication skills, persistence, patience, listening skills, etc., I can mention these qualities as aspects of fiction writing that have proven valuable to me.

Let's look at some examples relating to a fictional student named Pete Moss, a marketing student who lists his interests as follows: Photography, Camping, Skiing, and Volunteer Work. Check out some possible options for Pete if he's asked about his interests during a marketing interview:

"I see on your resume that you're interested in camping. Why does that interest you?"

Mediocre answer:	*"Yeah, I like to go up to Vermont once in a while. I guess that just being outdoors is what appeals to me. It's relaxing."*
Ordinary answer:	*"Yes, I try to go as often as I can in the summer. I find that it's a good way to clear my mind on the weekend, so I can return to work on Monday with a good focus."*
Extraordinary answer:	*"Besides being a relaxing way to recharge my batteries, camping is enjoyable to me because it requires a combination of characteristics: resourcefulness, good judgment, planning, stamina, and thinking on your feet. Some trips can be quite challenging, and I like to challenge myself."*

An employer who hears the first answer might wonder whether Pete can handle being indoors for six months! At best, this answer won't hurt you. The "Ordinary Answer" is better: It shows that Pete values a balance between work and other interests, and that he sees his weekend time as a way to be more energized in the workplace. However, the "Extraordinary Answer" reflects a job candidate who really "thinks marketing" and is able to make some subtle but creative connections between his career interests and his personal interests. With this answer, he never says anything directly about being a good candidate for the job, but the employer may start thinking that Pete's individual traits fit nicely with a marketing position.

But what if Pete had been asked about one of his other interests? Let's consider some options:

Photography:

"Photography appeals to my creative side, which is a very strong aspect of my personality. I also enjoy photography because I like the challenge of trying to capture something in a picture. It's like marketing, where you're trying to capture the nature of a product or service with one simple slogan or image. I like that."

Skiing:

"I haven't skied for very long—only three or four years—but I really enjoy everything about it. I like researching different ski mountains, finding out which appeals to me, and trying to sell my friends on which one I think is the best. On the mountain, I like taking on challenging terrain without sacrificing technique. I've improved very quickly."

Here we see two different approaches. In the photography example, Pete ties his interest in photography directly to its relevance in the field of marketing. In the skiing example, though, Pete is more subtle. He describes many aspects of skiing that are appealing to him, but the interviewer also can see that he's demonstrating many traits that are useful in a marketing job: researching, salesmanship, reasonable risk-taking, an outgoing personality, and a focus on results. The interviewer may be more likely to think of this student as a job candidate without even realizing why he or she feels that way!

Whatever your interests are, think about how you would talk about them if they come up in an interview. What connections can you make between your interests and a co-op position? If you can learn to do this well, an interviewer may be pleasantly surprised at your ability to turn a simple ice-breaker question into another showcase of your abilities.

3. *"Why should we hire you for this job?"*

If the interviewer has a more aggressive personality, you may hear this exact question in an interview. If not, you may find it in a more polite form (i.e., "What is it that makes you a good candidate for this job?"). In either case, the question an employer is *really* asking can be broken into many possible questions:

- How much self-confidence do you have?

- Are you a good match for this job?

- Do you *know* if you are a good match for this job?

- We expect you to sell our products or services, so how well can you sell yourself?

- Can you articulate your strengths clearly, confidently, and realistically?

Answer this question directly, focusing on your experiences, attitude, and aptitude in relationship to the job requirements as explained in the job description. In other words, don't just tell the employer why you're a good person, or a good candidate for *any* co-op job. Focus closely on why you are a good match for *this* co-op job. And if you don't have everything they're looking for in terms of skills, present a strategy for overcoming this obstacle.

Mediocre answer:	*"I've always wanted to work in this field, and I'm kind of intelligent. I think I could probably do a pretty good job."*
Ordinary answer:	*"I'm hard working; I have good grades; I'm eager to learn more, and I learn quickly. I also have good job experience that relates well to this position."*
Extraordinary answer:	*"According to the job description, you want someone who knows AutoCAD, and who has strong communication skills. In my class, I was the AutoCAD expert, and I help most of my friends with that and other software at school. As for communication skills, I encourage you to contact any of my previous employers. They'll tell you that I not only have excellent communication skills: I also was well respected by my colleagues on a personal and professional level. I also noticed that you prefer someone who has used Oracle. Since reading the job description, I've familiarized myself the basics of this program and am confident I could hit the ground running by the time this work period starts."*

The first answer gives the employer absolutely no incentive to hire the job candidate. Even worse, the candidate comes across as someone who has little or no confidence in himself/herself. The "Ordinary answer" is more positive, but it's rather generic: If an interviewer talks to ten students, this kind of answer will turn up three or more times. To stand out, you have to push your skills. In the "Extraordinary answer," the job candidate talks with confidence about past job experiences and shows a keen awareness of what the prospective job demands. If the employer didn't see these connections when looking at the resume, he or she will be clear on them now.

4. "What would you say are your strengths?"

This question makes some interviewees uncomfortable: People often don't like feeling that they are bragging about themselves, fearing that they will come across as egotistical. But remember: if you don't sell yourself in an interview, who will? Interviewers ask this question to assess your self-confidence, maturity, and self-awareness in addition to how well your strengths match up with the requirements of a job.

Here are a few guidelines to bear in mind when answering this question:

Be honest. On the one hand, don't exaggerate about your abilities. If you say you have a given technical skill, many employers will follow up with a question to assess how well your knowledge matches up with your claim. Or—if you do get hired by saying you have a skill when you actually don't—the truth will come out shortly after you start the job. Lying about your credentials is grounds for immediate dismissal with most employers.

On the other hand, be honest about what you *can* do. Many co-op candidates sell themselves short when asked about their strengths. If asked about their experience with computers, for example, many candidates will say they don't have any... overlooking the fact that they have taught themselves many software applications and, sometimes, even programming languages. Yes, self-taught skills count when you are asked about your strengths, skills, or experience in a given area.

Describe your strengths in terms of the employer's needs. One common mistake in answering this question is failing to tailor your reply to the employer's needs. Sure, your strengths may include fluency in Esperanto and Pig Latin, great speed in using a slide rule, and the ability to program in Pascal, but how are these skills going to help yourself as a candidate for a marketing position?

Before the interview, decide which of your strengths should be emphasized. If a telemarketing position primarily requires persuasiveness, excellent communication skills, and the ability to do straightforward mathematical calculations, you should strategize accordingly. In addition to citing examples of experience you've had that required persuasiveness, for example, you should plan on presenting yourself in an extremely persuasive manner. You also might cite a strong grade in a business statistics class. In contrast, you might not focus as heavily on your PC skills or your experience in marketing research. However, you might cite these skills heavily if interviewing for a position requiring these talents.

Let's consider some possible responses to the strengths question. Let's say that the job in question is a finance job requiring good experience with numbers, an ability to work as part of a team, and an understanding of how to calculate present values.

Mediocre answer:	*"I guess I'm a good worker, and I've done pretty well in most of my classes. I'm really good with computers too, especially spreadsheets and stuff."*
Ordinary answer:	*"I'm a real self-starter; I'm motivated and eager to learn. I got an A- in my finance class last semester, and I have excellent writing skills and presentation skills."*
Extraordinary answer:	*"I consider myself a real team player: I have no problem in doing any task that will help my team achieve our goals. I've always been a natural with numbers, although I do find a calculator is most effective for calculating present values. I learned about present values in my first finance class, and my ability to calculate them probably helped me earn an A- in the course."*

Although the second answer discusses many bona fide strengths which may help the candidate land a job somewhere, it goes into little detail regarding strengths that will prove beneficial to *this* employer. The extraordinary answer covers all of the areas mentioned in our mini-job description. Of course, this answer is only effective if the candidate is prepared to "walk the talk." A shrewd interviewer may follow up this question by giving the candidate a simple problem that requires the calculation of a present value. Be prepared to back up any claims that you make in an interview.

5. *"What are your weaknesses?"*
Less experienced interviewees dislike this question, probably because they're afraid of exposing a legitimate weakness that the interviewer will use against them in making a hiring decision. Or the interviewee may worry about giving an answer that really isn't an honest weakness, which may come off as an insincere response.

The good news is that this is not a difficult question to answer *as long as you are prepared to answer it*. You'll need to think it through beforehand because coming up with a good answer on the spot is quite challenging. Here are some basic guidelines in answering this question:

Start off your answer by acknowledging your strengths. You don't want to dwell on negatives more than necessary when answering this question, and you want to reinforce your strengths to make sure the interviewer understands them. One way to make sure you acknowledge your strengths is by starting your answer with "although" or "despite": "Although I have solid skill and experience in areas X, Y, and Z...."

Avoid cliché responses. Frequently, interviewees will cite "working too hard" or "being too focused on the job to the detriment of having a social life," etc. This kind of answer comes off as a cliché, at best, and insincere and defensive, at worst. In a way, you're telling the interviewer that you feel a need to dodge the question, as if you have something to hide.

Choose legitimate weaknesses, but not ones that would keep you from getting a job that you want. There are many ways to do this. If you are opposed to a job that would require 12 hours of work each day, you can describe your weakness as "I burn out if I have to work 60 hours a week on a regular basis." You can go on to explain that you get your work done efficiently, that your strength is in prioritizing, and that you have no objection to working long hours when necessary as long as it isn't every week. This kind of answer may keep you from getting a job... but it might be a job that you wouldn't have wanted anyway.

Keeping the job description in mind is also helpful when thinking up good weaknesses. If you're applying for a nursing job that requires good interpersonal skills, strong communication skills, and great attention to detail, your weakness could be the fact that your computer skills are limited to word processing and doing research on the Internet. Sure, you don't know databases, but you may not need to for this particular job. If you're a computer science student looking for a software development position, you probably wouldn't have a weakness such as shyness held against you. If a job description mentions the need for someone who is able to work independently with little supervision, you could discuss your inexperience in working with groups. If a job description mentions a hectic, unstructured work environment with unpredictable demands, you could state your weakness as follows: "I find that I tend to get bored easily if I'm forced to do the same job day in, day out. I don't deal with a steady routine and a rigid structure, which I find stifling and monotonous. So I think that would be a real weakness for me in some work settings." Of course, your weakness also needs to be an *honest* weakness.

Remember that you aren't expected to know everything. Perhaps the easiest way to deal with a question about your weaknesses is to acknowledge what the employer already knows about you: that is, admit that while you have a strong foundation of knowledge in your field of study, you still have a great deal to learn before you could be considered an expert in finance or computers or accounting or whatever. As long as you are enthusiastic and can convince the interviewer that you have aptitude for learning new skills, this kind of answer will work for you with most jobs. After all, you're applying for a job as a student or graduating senior who is in the process of learning a given field. As such, employers would expect that your learning is incomplete.

Emphasize what you have done or what you will do to improve your area of weakness. Who would you rather hire? A person who doesn't admit to having any weaknesses, or a person who tells you about a weakness and how he or she has worked to overcome it? This is a good strategy for anyone, but especially for students who struggle with the English language. Just saying that you're weak in English won't help you. However, if you explain that you have only been in this country for two years, and that you have been taking courses and practicing regularly to improve, and that you enjoy working on your English skills, you will impress some interviewers: most of whom know only one language!

Try to anticipate any concerns or perceptions employers have about your weaknesses as a job candidate. This ties in with the previous example about problems with speaking English. Most likely, an interviewer can tell if English is challenging for you, and he or she may wonder whether this will hurt your ability to do the job. You don't want the employer to be distracted with thoughts like this. So what you can do is bring up the concern yourself—maybe even in responding to a first question such as "Tell me about yourself." If you can anticipate the interviewer's concerns and eliminate them early in the interview, the interviewer is more likely to focus on your strengths.

One undergraduate business student does this very effectively in interviews. Due to a physical disability, this student needs metal crutches to help himself walk. The student knows that interviewers are probably curious about his disability but feel it would be impolite to ask him questions about it. And maybe they're wondering what's wrong with him: Would he be able to get around the workplace, for example?

The student figures that if the interviewer is thinking about his crutches, he or she is *not* giving him the attention he deserves as an individual. Maybe the interviewer isn't really listening to his carefully-prepared questions and answers. So right when the interview starts, the student says, "You're probably wondering why I'm on these crutches." He explains what happened (a motorbike accident), and he assures the employer that the disability doesn't keep him from being able to take a computer apart and put it back together again. Now the interviewer can focus on the student as a job candidate, not as a medical curiosity.

Let's consider some possible answers to "What are your weaknesses?"

Mediocre answer:	*"I don't really know anything about [sociology, journalism, accounting, etc.], and I don't really have any kind of real job experience."*
Ordinary answer:	*"I guess it would be that I work too hard. I forget to go to lunch, and the security guard has to ask me to*

> *leave at 10:00 each night, then I just sleep in my car so I can start working when the doors open at 6."*

Extraordinary answer: *"Although I have done extremely well in my sociology coursework, I would say my weakness is that I haven't yet had an opportunity to work directly in the field. Of course, that's hard to do without an advanced degree. But I hope to build on what I've learned in the classroom by honing my research and analytical skills and by getting some practical job experience in a human services position such as the one at your organization. There's always more to learn, and I can do so quickly."*

6. *"How are your grades?"*

If your grades are good, you probably won't be asked this question because your grade point average will be right on your resume. Obviously, the best solution to this question is to have good grades to begin with! If your grades are not good enough to put your GPA on your resume, though, you'd better be ready to answer this question.

Do employers care about your grades? Generally, yes. Admittedly, some don't care if your grades are mediocre as long as you can do the work. Others, however, may *require* a GPA of 3.0 or better, and others believe that grades are a good predictor of job performance. Right or wrong, this is the perception that you will need to overcome.

Once again, preparation will help you handle this type of question more effectively. Here are a few strategies that may prove helpful:

- *If your grades are good in the field for which you are applying, discuss those grades explicitly.* In other words, if you have a 2.4 GPA, but your grades in marketing classes are all Bs or better, then focus on those grades if you're applying for a marketing job.

- *If your GPA reflects one or two very low grades in a class outside of your major or concentration and/or in a class that may not relate to your success in this job, then say so.* Just be sure that the class *really* isn't relevant to the job at hand.

- *If your GPA reflects the fact that you need to work a significant number of hours during school to help pay tuition, then say so.*

- *If your grades have improved significantly over the last few quarters or semesters, acknowledge that you got off to a slow start but have improved significantly.*

Obviously, the best way to handle this question is to get good grades in the first place. Even though the statistical evidence shows that there is almost no relationship between grades and job success, employers don't necessarily know or believe that.

Anyway, here is the range of responses to "How are your grades?"

Mediocre response: *"Not too good. I have a 2.4."*

Ordinary response: *"Well, they're okay. I've done pretty well in classes in my major."*

Extraordinary response: *"Given that I've been working part-time while taking classes to help pay tuition, I think my grades are okay. When I take classes outside of my major, it's hard for me to put enough time into them. But my average in my psychology classes is a 3.2, so I think you'll find my academic background is strong in areas that will really count in this job."*

7. *"I see on your resume that you worked for Organization X last summer. What was that like?"*

Employers have much to gain by bringing up one or more of your previous job experiences. They want to:

- determine whether your experience at *that* job makes you a better candidate for *this* job.

- see how well you can articulate what another organization does and what your role was for that organization.

- see whether you have a positive attitude about previous work experience.

Keep these things in mind when working on an effective response to this question. Most interviewers will ask you about prior job experience, and you want to be ready for it. Follow these guidelines:

- *Describe what the organization does.* Unless the organization is very large or well known in its field, you may have to use a sentence or two to explain the nature of the work done by the organization. Show the interviewer you can capture the big picture of what a company does.

- *Describe what you did at the* organization. You probably did numerous things in your job at Organization X. Focus primarily on what you did well, what you enjoyed, and—most importantly—how it relates to the job for which you are currently interviewing.

- *Go beyond what is stated on your resume.* The interviewer can read, so you have to say more than what is written on your resume. This is why it is so important to tie your work experience to the description of the job for which you're applying.

- *ALWAYS focus exclusively on what was positive about the work experience.* Even if you hated your boss and found the job boring or unsatisfying, focus on the positives about the experience. Nobody likes a complainer or whiner, and the interviewer may start wondering if you might have significantly contributed to the problem and therefore would be a "risky hire."

Here are some responses interviewers might hear in response to "Tell me about your job at Organization X."

Mediocre answer:	*"Well, I did some pretty tedious office work: You know, answering phones, sending faxes, things like that. It wasn't much fun, and my boss was a pain, so I definitely want something different this time."*
Ordinary answer:	*"I worked for Organization X in Anytown for my last co-op job. I worked in an office and did a lot of administrative support work: xeroxing, answering phones, doing anything to help out the team."*
Extraordinary answer:	*"Organization X makes galvinators, which are electronic parts used in the automotive industry. I was an Office Assistant, responsible for handling clerical jobs in the Finance Department. The job was a good entry-level experience; the best thing about it was just having a chance to work alongside finance people and getting to pick their brains about the company's financial operations. That's why I'm interested in the position at your company: I'll get more exposure to the world of finance and get a chance to use some of the skills I've picked up in my finance classes over the last six months."*

Obviously, all three responses reflected a job that was not too demanding or exciting. The extraordinary answer, though, shows that you can be honest about this kind of job while still focusing on the positives of the experience.

Strategic Interviewing – An Employer's Perspective
by Steve Sim
If I can add any perspective on interviews, I'd have to say one thing: each and every experience you listed on your resume or talked about in an interview should have taught you something. Whether that lesson is how to do something right every time, or how to do something right the next time, it's a lesson learned. Be prepared to talk about it.
Steve Sim is a Technical Recruiter at the Microsoft Corporation.

8. *"Tell me what you liked LEAST about your job at Organization X."*

This request is basically a check of your attitude and your tact. Don't be tempted to bash your former boss, your co-workers, your lousy job, etc. Doing so will make you come off as a complainer or as someone who dislikes work.

For example, I interviewed a young woman for a medical writing job a few years ago. When I asked her about her previous job, she was only too happy to go on for a full 15 minutes about her horrible employer. Since this horrendous job was also in medical publishing, I finally put on a very concerned face and asked her "Do you think your previous experience has made you too bitter to continue to work in this industry?" She immediately realized her mistake, but it was too late. She had already been interviewed by our company president, who afterwards dismissed her with a simple sentence: "She's a whiner." We never did discuss her qualifications, which, actually, were quite good.

Instead of harping on the negatives, your best bet is to acknowledge that the job had many good aspects, but that you felt you wanted to broaden your experience and move on to something that would provide you with a bigger challenge.

Here are some sample responses for this request:

Mediocre answer:	*"They made me do all kinds of busywork that any idiot could do. Also, the pay was bad, my boss was totally clueless about how to manage me, and my co-workers were pretty useless, too.*
Ordinary answer:	*"It was an okay place to work, but it got kind of dull after awhile. And since I was just a co-op student, I had to do a lot of jobs that other people didn't want to do. Basically, it was just a way to make money for school."*
Extraordinary answer:	*"The job was definitely a good entry-level experience for me; I learned a great deal about _____, which I think will prove useful in my next job. I just believe that I could only learn so much in that job, so I decided it would be in my best interest to pursue something more challenging and interesting. That's why your job description caught my eye."*

9. *"Why did you choose Physical Therapy (or Communications, etc.) as your major?"*

An employer who asks this kind of question hopes to learn more about how focused, enthusiastic, serious, and mature you are. There are many good ways to answer this question, but there are also several bad ways. Thus, some helpful hints:

- *Show that you have a career plan.* You don't want it to sound like someone imposed the major on you, or that you're only majoring in it because some advisor or relative suggested it. Don't be vague when presenting your reasons. Relate the career plan to the job. If you have notions of going to law school, for example, don't talk about that option when you're dealing with a public accounting firm looking to recruit interns and co-ops after graduation.

- *Show some excitement.* One option is to tell the interviewer a short anecdote about what first excited you about economics, history, etc. You might mention a high-school job experience, a previous internship, a classroom experience, or some extracurricular activity that inspired you to major in your given concentration.

- *Make sure to connect your response to the interviewer's job description.* If you're seeking a job within your concentration, this should not be difficult. However, if you're pursuing a job in a different concentration or major, you are very likely to be asked about this discrepancy. Basically, if you're a psychology major, why are you interviewing for a job as a webmaster, for example? There may be plenty of good reasons, but you will need to make the connection. Otherwise, the employer may perceive a mismatch between you and the job.

Here are some sample answers for a student who is asked why he or she chose physical therapy as a major.

Mediocre Answer:	*"I dunno; I think it's kind of interesting. My dad says that the economy stinks for just about everything except the health sciences these days, so I figured it would be the best way to make a lot of money."*
Ordinary Answer:	*"I've always seemed to do well in my science courses, and I've enjoyed working with people in various jobs over the years. I think it's just a nice fit for my abilities."*
Extraordinary Answer:	*"I think I've always been a natural for the physical therapy field: Heck, I had to undergo physical therapy at the age of five, when I broke my arm falling off my bike. I'm great with people; I'm caring, and I really want to be in a healing profession that can help others in the way that I was helped as a child. I can't imagine another major that would fit so nicely with these qualities."*

What if someone is interviewing for a marketing job but actually majors in, say, communication studies? The interviewer may ask: "Given that your major is communications, why are you interested in a marketing position?"

Mediocre answer: *"Well, no one wanted to hire me for a communications job... ."*

Ordinary answer: *"I think it would be interesting, and it would give me broader experience in business in general."*

Extraordinary answer: *"I major in communication studies because there are many skills associated with it that I need to master to become a successful businessperson. I have the same interest in marketing, but I feel that many aspects of it—understanding the mentality of customers, knowing how to pitch to a specific market niche, and having a good mind for numbers and business—come naturally to me through my experiences in a family business. I decided I should use my college classes to improve on my weaknesses... not to build on what are already my strengths."*

10. *"What are your long-term career goals?"*
A variation on this one would be, "What do you see yourself doing in _____ years?" When employers ask this type of question, what they really want to know is many different things:

- *How focused or goal-oriented is the job candidate? Is she or he someone who plans ahead? Is she or he ambitious?* After all, you wouldn't want to hire someone who's just looking to make some quick cash, or someone who isn't achievement-oriented.

- *Does the job at hand really make sense as a match, given the job candidate's long-term goals?* If you're applying for a psychology position in an after-school program, but your long-term career goal is to become an entrepreneur, you had better be ready to explain why you're interested in the psychology job now. "I just really, really need a job" is not the best reason! It is entirely possible to explain the apparent disconnect, of course, but you have to give some thought as to how a job would fit into your career plan *before* you go out for that interview.

- *How mature and realistic is the candidate?* Your answer can reveal a great deal about your maturity and perception of yourself. If you don't have much of an answer, you may come off as someone who lacks focus and maturity. If you say that your goal is to someday be an administrative assistant, you may come off as lacking confidence or ambition. If you say that your goal is to be CEO of Microsoft, you may be seen as a dreamer, or as hopelessly naive... particularly if you have shown no initiative in acquiring computer skills.

89

That said, let's look at the range of replies an interviewer might hear to a question about long-term career goals. We'll assume that the student is interviewing for an entry-level bookkeeping job for a small company that manufactures furniture.

Mediocre answer: *"Well, I'm kind of undecided about that right now... I guess it would be to just pursue a job in my major after I graduate, then see what comes along."*

Ordinary answer: *"I hope to gain some valuable experience in accounting during my co-op jobs, then I'll pursue my CPA and see if I can get a job with a Big Five firm."*

Extraordinary answer: *"Down the road, I plan to get my CPA and work for a Big Five firm. I feel that the experience that I would gain from this opportunity would be very valuable, because an accountant needs to build good relationships with companies of all types and sizes. Working here would be give me an understanding and appreciation from that perspective, which is essential to success in public accounting."*

11. *"What kind of hourly rate are you looking for in this position?"*

The issue of pay can be an awkward matter in an interview. It's natural for you to be wondering about the pay rate or hoping for a specific figure, but your best bet is to not bring it up unless the employer does. And even then, you have to be careful about what you say. You don't want to get ruled out of a job for being greedy, but you don't want to accept $9.50 an hour when they would have been delighted to give you $12.

So how should you handle this question? First of all, always check the job description or ask the co-op coordinator what the pay rate is before you go in for an interview. If the job pays only $9.00 an hour, and you can't afford to take a job that pays less than $12.00, it's better to find out ahead of time rather than wasting everyone's time with an interview.

In many cases, the issue of pay in a co-op job is fairly rigid and non-negotiable. Some positions pay a certain figure, period. Others offer varied pay... but the pay only varies depending on your year in school; again, the pay rate is non-negotiable.

In some instances, however, the pay rate is a range that can vary depending on your skills, the employer's alternatives to hiring you, and your desirability as a candidate. The co-op coordinator will usually—but not always—have an accurate sense of what the realm of possibility is with pay. Find out before you go in for the interview.

If you *do* know what the pay rate or pay range is, you can acknowledge this in response to the question: *"My understanding is that the job pays something from $11 to $14 an hour, and I'd be comfortable with something within that range."*

This kind of response doesn't pigeonhole you as someone seeking a high or low pay rate and indicates that money isn't the most important consideration for you. For a co-op job, you never want to mention money as the reason you want a particular job, or as the main way you will decide between Job A and Job B.

If you *don't* know what the pay range or pay rate is, your best bet is to reply with a question: *"Is there a pay range that you have in mind for the position?"* Usually, there is, and many employers will provide you with a range. When you are told the range, it is best to not show any surprise, positively or negatively.

If you're pressed for a specific dollar figure, another option is to evade the question until an offer is presented: *"Money isn't the main factor in my decision. But I plan to interview with other companies, and if I get more than one excellent opportunity, then money could be an issue. But once you make me a specific offer, I will give you an answer within three business days."*

This kind of response indicates that money is not the top objective. More importantly, it helps you to project yourself as a person who has options and who considers himself or herself to be an attractive candidate. You want to show that you're strongly interested in the job, yes, but not desperate to get it!

Obviously, there are many other possible questions you might be asked in an interview. One accounting employer consistently asks job candidates to "define integrity." Some interviewers may ask candidates to name someone that they think of as a hero. We have heard of one employer who asked a job candidate to tell him a joke! In short, you cannot prepare for every specific question that you possibly could be asked.

But when you are asked an unusual question, don't panic: just think, how can I use this question to show that I am THE candidate who is the best MATCH for THIS job description. Whether you're defining integrity or describing your ideal job, this is something that you can focus on.

DEALING WITH DIFFERENT INTERVIEWER STYLES

Another challenge in preparing for an interview is that you may come across many vastly different interviewing styles. Sometimes, students return to the co-op office feeling frustrated because the interviewer never shut up and didn't really give them a chance to sell themselves. Others may be frustrated for the opposite reason: The interviewer barely talked at all, and they felt extremely awkward. So it may be useful to consider how to deal with different types of interviewers.

First of all, keep in mind that many interviewers are NOT experts in interviewing. They may not know the best questions to ask to determine how good a candidate you are. You may find this disappointing, but that's the way it goes. You may have to overcome an interviewer's weaknesses or personality if it keeps you from selling yourself. Here are some tips for dealing with several possible types of interviewers.

Type 1: "The Interrogator"

This interviewer likes to put job candidates on the spot. The Interrogator asks blunt questions, such as: "Why should we hire YOU for this job?" Or "What makes you think you know computers well enough to work here?" Alternatively, he or she may like to pose a challenge for you: "Here's a set of numbers. Figure out the present value of this sum of money if it's invested for 10 years at 8% interest." One interviewer likes to toss a beeper on the table and ask the potential MIS/finance co-op: "How would you go about developing a new operating system for this beeper?" Sales interviewers may pull out a 79-cent pen and say, "You have one minute to sell me this pen."

You should always be prepared for an intense interview. Assume that you're going to be challenged with difficult questions, and that you may be asked to back up your answers with a practical demonstration of your ability. In other words, be honest about what you can and can't do.

Most interviewers will not be this tough: particularly with co-op job candidates. Still, you have to be prepared for the possibility. And although many job candidates tremble at the thought of facing a high-pressure interviewer, the Interrogator is not the toughest to face. The Interrogator puts you under the microscope and evaluates how you handle tough questions or problems, but this gives you an opportunity to show how you can step up to a challenge and handle it.

Some of my MIS employers will just sit a student down at a computer and say, "Here's a broken computer—fix it." The interviewer sits and notes how the candidate attempts to tackle the problem as much as the result. As the following sidebar box indicates, this kind of "on the spot" challenge is not limited to business students.

Interviewer Types – An Engineering Co-op Perspective
by Bob Tillman
I do have some strong upper-class jobs that will only interview upper-class students. They want to know if you've had concrete design, if you've had steel design. Not only that, they'll want to see your transcript. I just had one of my former graduate students come back, and they gave him a test: Here's a beam—analyze it. That's the interview.
Bob Tillman is a cooperative education faculty coordinator
in Civil Engineering at Northeastern University.

Type 2: "The Buddy"

This interviewer is very different from the Interrogator. The Buddy will have more of a conversation with you about the job, asking questions in a non-threatening way, showing interest in who you are as a person, etc. Most students prefer this kind of interviewer, naturally, but you have to be careful. Some wily interviewers will intentionally take on this friendly tone because they know you are likely to let your guard down. With The Buddy, you might be likely to confide more of your weaknesses, shortcomings, and problems, because their friendliness seems so trustworthy. The Buddy will get you to admit that you got a C- in your accounting class—and will even sound sympathetic—then The Buddy will turn around and nail you when it comes time to pick the best candidate.

If the interviewer is casual and friendly, you should relax too: but be a little cautious. Don't ever forget that you're trying to sell your strengths and show why you're a good match for the job: even if you're doing this with a smile on your face and a more relaxed tone of voice. Friendly conversation can set a nice tone for an interview: Just make sure that your conversation gets beyond small talk.

Type 3: "The Nonstop Talker"

Although The Interrogator may sound like your worst nightmare, The Nonstop Talker is actually the most difficult type for most interviewees. You may sit through an interview that feels more like a lecture, barely getting a chance to say anything to this interviewer. At least The Interrogator gives you a chance to say something in your defense!

The Nonstop Talker may not be immediately recognizable. Many good interviewers will begin by telling you a great deal about the job and the organization before asking you questions. The Nonstop Talker may talk about these things, too, in addition to himself or herself, the previous co-op student that worked at the company, and a whole bunch of other topics. The next thing you know, the interviewer has used up all of the scheduled time, and you've done little but nod a lot. Of course, this is a low-pressure interview, but you run the risk of coming across as part of the office furniture: In other words, this type of interview may mean that they like you and have basically decided to hire you, but it also may mean that you are completely forgotten by the interviewer.

When interviewed by The Nonstop Talker, you have to walk a fine line: Don't interrupt, but DO take advantage of any break in the monologue by asking a question that brings the Talker around to considering you as a candidate. During a pause, you might be able to politely say: "Can I ask you a question? I'm very interested in this job. What would be useful for you to know in order to find out whether I'm the best candidate for the job?" Another strategy is to acknowledge and flatter The Talker's talking while changing the focus of the talk: "I've certainly learned a great deal about you, this job, and the organization. In fact, from what you've said, I think this opportunity would be a great match for my skills because...." At this point, you can tailor your response to what you've learned from the nonstop talking... as long as you were listening carefully!

In short, try to get The Nonstop Talker to focus on you. He or she may still talk a great deal, but at least it might be about you and your ability to do the job.

Type 4: "Silent But Deadly"

This interviewer is the opposite of the talker, but this style can be equally frustrating. The Silent But Deadly interviewer will ask very few questions, and the questions may be very vague or general. So why is this interviewer potentially "deadly?" Basically, he or she gives nervous job candidates every opportunity to hang themselves! Consider the following dialogue:

Interviewer:	*So... tell me about your weaknesses.*
Job Candidate:	*Although I have a good understanding of basic accounting from classwork and my first co-op job, I need to learn more in order to master accounting: specifically, I'm looking forward to learning more about taxes, which is why the job with your company appeals to me.*
Interviewer [nods slowly]:	*Hmmmm......*
Job Candidate:	*Um, and I guess you want another weakness?*
Interviewer [nods]:	*Uh-huh...*
Job Candidate:	*Hmmm.... okay, let me think... Um, I guess I'm not that strong when it comes to debits and credits.... I get my ledger entries confused sometimes...*
Interviewer [nods, says nothing]:	
Job Candidate:	*And.... I suppose that getting a C+ in my last accounting class wasn't that strong.*

Do you see what can happen in this situation? The job candidate started off with a strong answer but then interpreted the interviewer's silence as a negative: The candidate assumed that he or she failed to answer the question adequately. As a result, the candidate supplied more information. In this case, it was information that can only hurt the individual's chances of getting a job.

Most Silent But Deadly interviewers act this way because it reflects their personalities. But some shrewd interviewers may use this as a deliberate strategy to see if you will hang yourself if given enough rope. This is especially common when asking about weaknesses or reasons for leaving a previous job or situation.

Either way, your strategy is simple. If the length of the silence starts to feel awkward, ask a clarifying question: "Does that answer your question?"; "Is there anything else you'd like to ask me?"; "What else would you like to know about me?" Unless you're asked a specific question requesting more information, have faith in your answer; don't assume that silence or apparent indifference means that you have to say something more.

During my last job search, I was interviewed by a very quiet, introverted gentleman. After each of my answers, he would let a solid ten seconds go by; once, he waited for a good 20 seconds, as if he were curious to see how I would handle that. But I believed I had given a strong, definitive answer, so I simply waited. Finally, he said, "Is there anything you'd like to add?" I replied, pleasantly, "What else would you like to know?" Ultimately, I was offered the job. Of course, if I were interviewing for a marketing position, I probably would have needed to be more aggressive in that situation. So it just goes to show you: There is seldom one "right" way to handle an interviewing challenge. It's always difficult to feel that you need to carry both sides of any conversation. But if you can take charge of the situation by offering to explain why you're a good match for the job, what you have to offer the organization, and by asking questions that reflect your research, you may succeed in bringing this interviewer out of his or her shell.

Type 5: "The Big Picture Person"
This interviewer is prone to asking very open-ended, general questions, such as:

- Tell me about yourself.

- What do you want to do with your life?

- What are your career goals?

- What kind of person are you?

Students often don't like these questions because there seems to be no clear-cut way to answer them. Again, though, remember the rule: When asked about something *general*, answer in a way that shows why you are a match for this *specific* job. What kind of person are you? "I'm the kind of person who has a great deal to offer to a small medical office like this one. I have excellent grades in my anatomy and physiology classes, and I have solid experience working hands-on with people as a volunteer at the small hospital in my hometown. If you hire me, you will be employing a person who has a solid base of experience as well as someone who picks up new things quickly and does work without complaining." If that's the kind of job description in question, that's the right kind of specific answer to a "big picture" question.

Type 6: "The Human Resources Interviewer"
If you are interviewed by someone in an HR department, you may or may not be asked questions relating to your technical skills. An experienced HR person may have enough expertise to ask you about specific tasks, but it is not uncommon to come across an HR interviewer who knows little about engineering, nursing, or social work. Alternatively, the HR interviewer may have the knowledge but decide that such questions are better left to the person who would be your

supervisor if you're hired. Either way, the HR interviewer is more likely to ask the classic interview questions as described in the previous section. The questions may be more "warm and fuzzy," as the purpose of this interview may be to "screen" candidates to determine who will go on to the next phase of the interview process. Be prepared for a structured interview, and don't get too technical in your responses unless the interviewer seems to be looking for that. Save your more technical answers for the interviewer who is a network administrator or mechanical engineer—someone who is an expert in your field, whatever it is.

Interviewer Types – A Health Sciences Co-op Perspective
by Rose Dimarco

Nursing could be different than physical therapy in that nursing may have people in Human Resources to interview you; they may have nurse recruiters interview you. Part of their skill base is knowing how to interview. In physical therapy, you're more apt to be interviewed by the physical therapist—who may have zero skills in interviewing. So if you're going to probably be interviewed by someone who doesn't know how to interview you that well, what do you want to have them remember about you before you walk out? That means when they're walking you down the hall, and they're showing you all the equipment and all the treatment rooms, how are you going to script what you want to say so that you interject what is it about you that you think would fit? If you're being interviewed by someone in Human Resources, and they're more skilled in interviewing, it might be more traditional questions: Tell me about yourself, what are your strengths and weaknesses?

You have to decide: What three things do I want them to remember about me? It's not: 'Oh, what a cute guy—he's trying to get through school; his mom and dad had three jobs.' It's not that kind of remembrance: It's remembrance about what value you bring, and those three things you have to somehow interject. As they talk about things, don't be afraid to say "That reminds me of when I was in high school, and I had to work under pressure because I had x, y, and z to do, and here's how I dealt with it."

Rose Dimarco is a cooperative education faculty coordinator in Physical Therapy at Northeastern University.

Type 7: "The Behavioral-Based Interviewer"

Some organizations swear by the Behavioral-Based Interviewing (BBI) approach, and for good reason: Studies have shown that this style is generally more effective in determining whether someone is a good match for the job. In particular, Big Five accounting firms such as Deloitte and Touche and PricewaterhouseCoopers often use this approach. Microsoft and other corporations also may use these questions to determine if you have specific "core competencies" that are considered to be vital to success at the organization in question: drive/results orientation; passion for learning; ability to work in a team; ability to handle conflict effectively; good ethical judgment; etc.

The behavioral-based interview features questions that require specific stories in response. This makes it much more difficult for the interviewee to come up with a slick-sounding, canned answer: Instead, he or she must recount something that they really experienced in the classroom or at work. In answering, the interviewee is urged to walk the interviewer through the specific situation and to detail what they were thinking, feeling, and doing in dealing with it.

Here are some typical BBI questions:

- Tell me specifically what your greatest accomplishment in life thus far has been.

- Tell me about a time when you had to overcome a challenge or obstacle when working as part of a team.

- Tell me about a time when you felt really successful in something at work.

- Describe a situation in which you faced an ethical dilemma and how you dealt with it.

If you're not too forthcoming or struggle initially, the interview may add, "Just walk me through what was going on step-by-step..." or something like that.

The key to these interviews is to have several good, specific stories that you are ready to share. Think long and hard ahead of time about which stories will best showcase your positive qualities—some stories are better than others! Describe the situation specifically first, then logically walk the interviewer through how you handled the situation step-by-step, wrapping up with a description of what ended up happening due to your actions.

Practice the telling of your behavioral-based stories ahead of time. Last summer, my nephew interviewed for an engineering position—his first job out of college. Ahead of time, they gave him a list of core competencies that they seek in applicants and told him that they would be looking for him to share some personal experiences related to those competencies. I told him that this was like going for a test where you have been given the questions a week in advance! However, the first time he told me his stories, they weren't good enough. He had to try out some stories to figure out which ones would be the BEST stories to showcase his strengths. After extensive practice and preparation—and despite limited internship experience—he went in and nailed the interview, and it turned out to be the only offer he got in a tough economy. Without strategizing and practicing for a behavioral-based interview, it may not have happened.

Whether or not you ever have a behavioral-based interview, having extremely vivid and specific examples to share is always a smart idea: It brings alive your ideas and tells employers what you *really* mean when you say that you can learn quickly or work independently or be a strong team player.

Type 8: "The Olympic Judge"

The Olympic Judge likes to let you know how you're doing throughout the interview. As you might imagine, this can be encouraging, disconcerting, or both. This interviewer may come out and say, "Good answer!" However, this individual may also shake his head or frown or say, "Well, I don't know if that's what we're looking for."

Dealing with immediate negative feedback can be very challenging to your confidence. How can you handle it? Most importantly, *don't ignore it*. If an interviewer reacts negatively to one of your answers, ask a clarifying question: "Is there a concern you have about that answer?" Once you understand why the interviewer reacted negatively, try to acknowledge the concern and address it as best as you can. For example, if you're asked to cite your experience in marketing research, and the interviewer reacts negatively to your response, you might handle it like this:

Job candidate:	*I noticed that you had a negative reaction to my answer. What is it about my research experience that concerns you?*
Interviewer:	*Well, my sense is that your experience is good but extremely limited.*
Job candidate:	*I think it's fair to say that the quantity of experience I've had is limited. But I feel that the quality of experience has been outstanding. My position at Galvinators Unlimited gave me a great opportunity to gain exposure to research..."*

The candidate could then go on to tout some specifics about this research experience. Would this be enough to turn around the Olympic Judge's perception? Maybe not, but it would at least give you a chance. It shows assertiveness, desire to get the job, and sensitivity to the concerns of others.

A variation on the Olympic Judge interviewer is the person who asks *you* to judge yourself: "On a scale of 1 to 10, with 1 being terrible and 10 being fantastic, how would you rate yourself in terms of...." The interviewer then asks you to rate your communication skills, your analytical ability, your interpersonal skills, etc.

This kind of question tests your honesty, realism, and savvy: Rating yourself uniformly high comes off as insincere or unaware, but who will hire you if you give yourself low ratings? When answering this question, make sure you do yourself justice, but make sure to rate yourself lower in certain areas: particularly those that seem less related to the job that you want. Don't rate yourself as a 1 or 2 in something unless you really know nothing about it (i.e., you're asked about C++ programming, and you've never done anything like it). For most generic characteristics, stick between 6 and 10. Bear in mind that your coordinator would not send your resume out for a position if he or she believed that your skills were not a reasonable match for the given job. Have confidence in your skill level, and show it with ratings that are realistic and positive.

TURNING THE TABLES: ASKING THE RIGHT QUESTIONS DURING AN INTERVIEW

Many job candidates think of interviewing as an audition for a part. This perception has some truth to it, but it's not the whole story. In an interview, you *are* trying to show that you're the best person for the job. Additionally, though, you're trying to determine whether the job is a good match for you. In that sense, interviewing should be a two-way street.

The nice thing about asking questions in an interview is that it helps to achieve both of these goals. Asking smart questions is a great way to show the interviewer that you are:

- prepared for the interview in terms of researching the job and the company.

- excited about the job.

- determined to find out whether *you* think this job is the best match for your considerable talents.

Interviewing – An Employer's Perspective
by Mike Naclerio
The goal of interviewing is to determine a "mutual" fit between the company and potential employee. Too often, candidates view interviews as situations where they have to prove to a company that they are good enough to fit in. They often overlook the opportunity they have to "interview the company" to see if the company is good enough for them (i.e., does the company have an appropriate level of ethics, will the position be satisfying, what type of people work there, etc.). So, candidates should not lose sight of this opportunity and ask questions!
Mike Naclerio is the Director of Relationship Management at the workplace HELPLINE.

All of these things reflect favorably on you as a job candidate. Likewise, asking questions is a great way for the interviewer to show you whether:

- the job is what it appears to be in the job description.

- the job is something that you will be excited about doing for several months (or at least one year if it's a full-time post-graduation position).

- the job is indeed a good match for someone with your level of skills.

Don't underestimate the importance of determining whether the job is what you really want. *More often than not, individuals who end up disliking their jobs failed to ask the right questions during the interview.* Basically, they didn't have a realistic sense of what the job requirements would be. As a result, they end up being bored or overwhelmed. But isn't it the employer's fault for failing to communicate this to the job candidate, you might say? True, a great interviewer will do this effectively. However, if an interviewer fails to do so, it's your responsibility to ask if you want to ensure that misunderstandings are avoided.

What questions should I ask?

Many internship and co-op candidates—even many experienced professionals— struggle to come up with good questions. When they are given the opportunity to ask questions during an interview, they will to try think up some on the spot, then decline the opportunity.

Like so many things in interviewing, this element requires preparation. You should have as many as eight to ten questions ready to ask before you even arrive for the interview. Why so many? Because several questions that you had beforehand may be answered during the course of the interview. Most interviewers won't simply ask questions; they'll talk a little about the company and explain a little more about the job. Thus, you need to have numerous questions ready.

What are the "best" questions to ask? In my opinion, the best questions are the ones that:

- force the interviewer to imagine you in the job.

- reflect your attitude and values positively.

Let's consider what this means. If you want the job, it is certainly in your best interest to make the interviewer imagine you in the job. You can do this by using the words "I," "me," and "my" in your question. For example:

- *What would my typical day be like in this position?*

- *Who would train me when I begin this job?*

- *Would I receive regular feedback about my performance?*

These are good questions, but the very best ones are those which also reflect a positive attitude and strong values. Consider these:

- *What could I do between now and the first day of co-op to be ready to hit the ground running in this job?*

- *It's important to me to get an outstanding evaluation in my co-op job: What could I do to really stand out as an exceptional employee in this job?*

- *I definitely want a job that challenges me and keeps me busy. Given that, can you give me a sense about whether this position would be right for me?*

- *I would be glad to work part-time after the co-op ends. Do you think that's a possibility?*

- *If I excel in this job, would I be able to have more responsibilities added to my job description?*

Here are some other good questions:

- *What would you say is the most challenging part of this job?*

- *In the research that I did to prepare for today, I noticed that your company is trying to (i.e., implement a new marketing strategy, adopt a new process of providing quality care to patients). How has this development changed things in this department?*

- *This job involves several different responsibilities: Which do you think would require most of my time?*

- *Why do YOU like working for this company?*

- *If everything works out well for this co-op period, would it be possible for me to work here in the future?*

- *How often do you hire co-ops on a full-time basis after they graduate?*

Asking these kinds of questions will show the interviewer that you are serious about the job, and that you value yourself highly enough to know that other options may be more attractive to you than this one. Because this is true, you need to see if the company meets your needs as well as you meet theirs.

ENDING ON A HIGH NOTE

If you have ever taken a psychology class, you may have heard of a phenomenon called the primacy/recency effect. Research has shown that when individuals are presented with a significant amount of information, they tend to best remember what they are exposed to first and last; the middle tends to get hazy.

We already discussed how to get off to a good start. Now let's discuss how you can cap your interview with a strong ending. Here are a few basic guidelines:

Take charge of the transition from asking questions to closing the interview.

Don't wait for the employer to figure out that you have no more questions to ask. The best approach is to bridge from asking questions into closing the interview. After you've had your job-related questions answered, simply say: "I have just one more question. When do you plan to make a hiring decision?"

Ask the interviewer what the next steps will be.
After you learn when the decision will be made, ask the interviewer what his or her preference is regarding next steps: "Would you like me to call you next week about the decision, or should I just wait to hear from you?" If the interviewer says that you can call, make sure to get a business card, or, at least, a phone number you can call.

Thank the interviewer for taking the time to meet with you.
Even if you're not interested in the job, be graceful and polite. Acknowledge the fact that the interviewer has devoted part of his or her day to talk to you. Show some appreciation for the experience, and mention something specific about your conversation that was enlightening. One possibility would be: "Thank you for taking the time to meet with me today. I learned a great deal about the nursing practices in a geriatric care facility. I look forward to hearing from you."

Shake the interviewer's hand before leaving, and make sure that you haven't left behind any personal belongings.

If you have any doubts about whether or not you handled questions well, write them soon after you leave. Then you can discuss them with your coordinator.

AFTER THE INTERVIEW: FOLLOW-UP STEPS

To some degree, your follow-up steps may vary depending on the employer's needs or preferences. In all circumstances, respect any request that an employer makes of you, whether it's getting a writing sample to her or additional references to him, calling on a particular day, or not calling at all.

Most people would agree that writing a thank-you note or letter or e-mail would be appropriate at this point. However, make sure that any such note or letter is absolutely perfect in terms of grammar and spelling... especially when writing the name of the manager or organization. Sending no thank-you letter at all is better than sending one with errors.

Keep your thank-you note simple and professional. A safe approach would include the following steps:

- *Thank the interviewer for taking the time to meet with you on Thursday (or whatever day it was).*

- *Say something positive about the interviewing experience: something you found especially intriguing to learn about the company, its products/services, the job, etc.*

- *Briefly reinforce your interest in the position (if you have any) and why you would be a good match for the position.*

- *Encourage the interviewer to contact you if any additional information is needed.*

A pleasant and timely thank-you note can't turn a mediocre candidate into a great one. But it can make all the difference if the employer is struggling over the decision or believes that several candidates could do the job.

SPECIAL CONSIDERATIONS FOR MARKETING INTERVIEWS

Generally, most of the information that you have read so far can prove useful when interviewing for any job. As we also have alluded to, however, there are some critical differences between marketing interviews and those for jobs related to other majors.

Why are marketing interviews different? Frequently, marketing employers expect a more aggressive approach. Since sales and marketing are closely related, the marketing employer will closely examine your ability to sell yourself: If you can't persuasively sell yourself in an interview, they believe, how can you be expected to sell that company's products and services? You really have to prepare your "interview presentation" with this in mind. Here are some tips:

- *Generally, it is a good idea to bring notes to a marketing presentation.* As noted earlier, this would be a real no-no for many interviews, but many marketing employers believe that a *lack* of notes reveals a lack of preparation. Thinking on your feet is one thing, but "winging it" for an important presentation is another one entirely! A short section on how to prepare and use notes can be found on page 105.

- *Be aggressive.* There is no room for shyness in a marketing presentation. Your self-presentation should be energetic, persuasive, and geared toward pushing the employer for a commitment.

- *Ask for the job.* Again, this is something you would not do with most non-marketing employers. But in a marketing interview, conclude your sales pitch with an attempt to close the deal. Your ability to close this deal may reflect your aggressiveness in closing in a selling situation on the job. If you want the job, ask for it. If you can do the job, tell them.

- *Seek closure.* At the end of a marketing interview, ask the interviewer when they expect to make a decision regarding the position. Keeping this information in mind, it is generally recommended that you follow up with the employer after your interview. Be aware that there is a fine line between being persistent and being a pain in the neck. Some marketing students have failed to get jobs because they failed to follow up with interviewers. Others have been turned down because they called too many times and alienated the interviewer.

Interviewing – A Student's Perspective
by Gabriel Glasscock

As expected, your first few interviews will be a little nerve-wracking. But that's to be expected. It's impossible to know exactly the type of interviewer you will have. So try not to prepare too much for a certain type of interviewer. Rather, invest your time into knowing as much about the job as possible. Find good potential conversation starters. I found it good to start a conversation on relevant job-related topics (where appropriate). This shows the employer that you are not just interested in the job but the field as a whole, and it also eases some of the tension. Look them in the eye, and use good body language.

Expect the unexpected. One time, I was at Snell Library at 8:30 p.m. in the middle of an intense group session. I got a call from a recruiter for an excellent position in Florida with a Big Five firm. We had been playing phone tag for a few weeks and she was to make a decision the next day on whom to hire: I had to interview over the phone outside the library in the freezing cold of December. I knew this would be my one and only 15-minute chance at this job, and I had to sell myself RIGHT THEN, without any preparation at all. Unlike most interviews, this was not pre-arranged: The interviewer wanted to see how well I could think on my feet.

The main thing is self-confidence. They were looking for a trainer in Java. When she asked the infamous "Why should we hire you?" question, I had to be creative. Although I had no prior experience with Java, I convinced her that my experience with Visual Basic would help greatly with learning Java, as both are object-oriented programming languages. Understanding transferable skills—and knowing how to use and express them—is an essential quality for an interviewee and also one of my favorite parts of this guidebook.

Any time an interviewer gives you the floor to ask questions, ASK QUESTIONS. Always have several prepared. I used the "Why do you like working here?" question with the Big Five recruiter, and she loved talking about that. Ask questions that show you have an interest in working there in your specific job and in being a part of their company.

Gabriel Glasscock was an MIS student at Northeastern University, Class of 2002.

Accordingly, remember these guidelines:

- *After making clear that you want the job and can do it, ask when a hiring decision will be made.* This will help you plan your follow-up efforts accordingly.

- *If the interviewer tells you when you should call back to follow up, honor their wishes.* If they tell you not to call until next week, then wait until next week.

- *Don't be a pest.* Job candidates have sometimes lost jobs because they kept calling until the employer got fed up with it. Unless you're told otherwise by your coordinator or a potential employer, limit follow-up calls to one or two per week.

- *Remember that the policy of following up after an interview often doesn't apply if you're interviewing for non-marketing jobs.* Some marketing students pursuing opportunities in finance, accounting, etc. have come across as pushy and obnoxious by repeatedly calling interviewers. If you are interested in opportunities outside of marketing, remember that the recommended follow-up procedure is to simply send a thank-you letter to the interviewer(s).

In any job interview, of course, you need to sell yourself persuasively. In a marketing interview, though, you can do so much more directly. But again, remember this warning for marketing majors who apply for non-marketing jobs: Be sure to tone down your presentation, or you may be perceived as pushy, arrogant, or obnoxious. As always: If in doubt, ask the coordinator who works with the employer about what approach would be most effective.

USING NOTES IN INTERVIEWS

As mentioned above, using notes in marketing interviews is strongly recommended. Additionally, though, students in other concentrations may find this to be a helpful idea. The single best thing about notes is that they are a safety net if you are concerned about "going blank" due to negative nervous energy. Your notes will not include word-for-word answers, but they will feature enough words to jog your memory if you blank out. And if you don't go blank at all, nothing says that you HAVE to use them just because you prepared them.

But what if an employer questions you on why you are using notes? Simply say that this interview is important to you and that it is important for you to feel prepared: You wanted to make sure that you got across everything that mattered in terms of why you are a good fit for the job.

How should your notes look? One former colleague suggests having your notes on an 8 ½ x 11-inch piece of paper, which is divided into four quarters:

- One quarter features key strategic points you intend to make about why you are a good match for the job. For example: "Excellent ability to work in a team." Beneath each point, you might write words to help you remember a specific example that shows that strength in action (i.e., Example: Crazy day working at Banana Republic on Friday after Thanksgiving).

- One quarter has key notes about the job or company that you learned by researching the position.

- One quarter has eight or ten questions that you might ask, so you can be sure that all of your questions won't be answered in the course of the interview.

- The last quarter is left blank, so you can use it to take notes on what the interviewer says during the interview.

I suggest either writing your notes in large print or—if on computer—printing them out in a large font, so that they are easy enough to read without having them leave your lap or a tabletop. Make sure that you don't wave your notes around. Keeping them on one piece of paper will help you from fumbling around during the interview to find what you need. A portfolio can be handy when using notes: You can buy one which has a flap for your resume and references on one side, with a clipboard for your one page of notes on the other side. Hand over a fresh resume and references when sitting down, then fold over the portfolio so your notes page is right in front of you.

HANDLING JOB OFFERS

Right now, you might believe that the least of your problems is how to deal with job offers. Just *getting* a job offer may seem improbable for the time being. However, your job situation can change quickly, and you need to know how to handle job offers. In recent months, I just can't believe how many times an employer has called to tell me that they offered a job to someone, only to have the response be a low-energy mumble, indicating only that the person would have to think about it. In extreme cases, I have seen an employer pull back an offer in this situation, figuring that they don't want to hire someone who only wants the job as a last resort.

So don't take this small step for granted! Here are some quick tips.

Be proactive.
As soon as you get home after an interview, you should write down the pros and cons of accepting a job offer with that company. Without thinking about any other options that you may or may not have, is this a job that you would accept? In other words, start making up your mind BEFORE you get the offer.

ALWAYS start out by thanking the person for making you the job offer.
If someone is not sure if they want to accept a co-op job, they often quickly state that they'll have to think about it or that they aren't sure. This is impolite, at best. You should be flattered to receive ANY job offer: whether or not you choose to accept it. You also may mention some aspect of the interview that you found enjoyable.

EXAMPLE: *"First, I'd like to thank you for offering me this position. I enjoyed getting the chance to hear what you had to say about working for [ORGANIZATION]."*

AFTER thanking them, gracefully tell them what your situation is.
If you definitely know whether or not you want the job, AND you're clear about the position and pay, this will be easy. The hard part is knowing what to say

when you're really not sure what to do or if the job is good but not necessarily your top choice. I suggest handling this situation carefully: You don't want to treat any employer like a second or third choice, but you also don't want to give someone the impression that you probably will take a job when you don't feel that way. Also, you have to be sensitive to the employer's needs. It's not fair to keep an offer dangling for weeks while you make your mind; if you ultimately say "no," then the employer will miss out on other good students. Most coordinators at my university believe that you should make up your mind within THREE BUSINESS DAYS OF RECEIVING AN OFFER. In other words, if a company makes you an offer on Thursday, you will need to say yes or no by the following Tuesday.

Here is the simplest way to keep an offer on hold without making a potential employer feel like you're shopping around for something better:

EXAMPLE: *"I promised my co-op coordinator that I would discuss things with her (or him) before making a final decision, but I definitely will get back to you in no more than three business days, and sooner than that if possible."*

Here is another way to keep an offer on hold without alienating a potential employer:

EXAMPLE: *"Let me tell you what my situation is: I'm considering a few other employers right now, and I want to be fair to those other employers and give them a chance to make me an offer. But I WILL give you my decision within three business days, and sooner than that if possible. Is that okay?"*

An employer has every right to ask you to make a decision faster if possible. However, you also have the right to talk to your coordinator before saying yes or no. If you feel that an employer is trying to corner you into making an on-the-spot answer, let your coordinator know. This generally does not happen and should not happen.

Be clear on what you are being offered.
If the employer has not told you what your hourly pay rate would be, NOW is the time to ask or to confirm what you believe the pay rate to be. Do so before you accept the job to avoid any misunderstandings. Likewise, you should be clear on what hours and days they expect you to work, your start date and end date, and what your responsibilities will be, so everyone is clear about this.

Be careful about pay rate issues.
In many cases, the pay rate will not be open to negotiation: You should know whether or not it is before you bring up the matter. And even if there is some room for negotiation, there are some good reasons to avoid doing so: Pushing for more pay can send the message that you care more about the money than about the learning experience.

When there is some room for negotiation, you probably should not take matters into your own hands. Talk to your coordinator to find out if there is any latitude regarding pay. In some rare cases, a coordinator may be able to negotiate a higher pay rate. This takes skill and experience, however, as handling this the wrong way can backfire quickly.

The same is true in cases when you are offered less than the job description indicated or less than your coordinator told you to expect. If this occurs, thank the employer for the offer, tell him or her that you need to talk to your coordinator before reaching a final decision, and contact your coordinator immediately about the situation. Perhaps the situation has changed, or the company simply has made a mistake. Either way, get your coordinator's advice before proceeding on your own.

If you're not sure what to do, contact your co-op coordinator immediately.

It's hard to predict every dilemma that you may face when getting a job offer. But if in doubt about what to do, seek the advice of your coordinator. In some cases, a coordinator may be able to get a faster response from a second employer if you need to make a decision about an offer from a first employer within three business days. If it's a matter of indecision, your coordinator probably will not tell you what to do: She or he may try to help you walk through the different pros and cons of the offer or offers. In the end, though, it's your decision.

ALWAYS be polite when turning down a job offer.

Usually, people feel awkward when they have to turn down a job. This is understandable: Employers may be very disappointed to hear about your decision. But usually they understand if you are professional and gracious about it (see the sidebar box).

EXAMPLE: *"I just wanted to let you know that I decided to accept a job with another company. It was a tough decision: I just felt that this other job was a slightly better match for me in my current situation. But I do appreciate your offer, and I hope that you can find a good candidate for your position."*

Declining A Job Offer – A Health Sciences Co-op Perspective
by Rose Dimarco

A student who was in her third year interviewed for a job and she got it, but she felt she was more compatible with a very different experience, so she turned it down. But she sent a thank-you note—even though she rejected the offer. She praised that employer—she did not want to burn that bridge.

It turned out that she eventually interviewed again with that employer. It was the same interviewer, and she remembered—very positively—that rejection. So she ended up with a second chance at the job.

Rose Dimarco is a cooperative education faculty coordinator in Physical Therapy at Northeastern University.

Follow up with ALL employers once you have made a decision.
After you have made a timely decision, make sure that you communicate that decision to EACH employer that is waiting to hear as well as to each co-op coordinator that you have worked with to obtain the job.

Once you have accepted a job offer, you CANNOT go on other interviews or consider other job offers.
There are NO exceptions to this rule. Think of it this way: Accepting a job and continuing to interview is like getting engaged and continuing to go on dates. It doesn't make sense, and it's just plain wrong. Or, if you'd like to think of it another way, how about this: How would you feel if a company makes you an offer on November 1st, you accept the offer and stop pursuing other jobs; maybe you even turn down another good job or two. A week or two later, the company calls you up and tells you "Sorry, but somebody else came along who turned out to be a better candidate." Universities would not work with an employer who behaved in this way, and, likewise, career professionals will not work with you if you treat an employer in a similar way.

That said, you absolutely SHOULD call back any employer who is interested in interviewing you, even after you have accepted a job. It's professional and courteous to follow up on any interview request, and it is not hard to get across the situation: "I wanted to thank you for your interest in interviewing me. However, I have accepted a position with another employer, so I am no longer available. But I do wish you luck in finding a good candidate, and I will keep you in mind for a future co-op job."

Once you have accepted the offer, make sure to see your co-op coordinator one last time.
Let your coordinator know as soon as you have a job lined up: That's why 24-hour voice mail exists. Your coordinator generally will ask you to come in to complete an agreement form and to go over success factors for your position.

DRUG TESTING

It's important to know that some employers make offers that are contingent upon the candidate's ability to pass a drug test successfully. Though many employers do not require this, drug testing is on the rise. Two of my large and prominent co-op employers—The Gillette Company and General Electric—require drug testing for all new hires. Eventually you're likely to encounter this issue.

Why do companies drug test? People with substance abuse problems can be costly to organizations in terms of absenteeism, tardiness, and turnover. Companies don't want invest time, money, and energy developing a co-op or new employee who may not prove to be a productive worker.

If you do use illegal drugs—or if you use any prescription drugs *without* having a prescription—you may have time to change your behaviors. Many companies now use hair tests to test for drug use—these tests are harder to fool than urine tests. These tests generally will reveal if you have regularly used drugs over the last three or four months. If you're a fall semester sophomore and stop using drugs now, you likely will be able to pass a drug test for a summer/fall job. If you don't want to limit your opportunities, you should consider this choice carefully.

In some fields, drug testing is not just a part of the hiring process—it's an ongoing part of being a professional employee. See the sidebar box below: It's a good example of a situation in which a couple of good students were wise enough to recognize that they'd better not interview for a position for this reason. These situations should lead you think about if you need to make a lifestyle choice—unless using drugs illegally is more important to you than being eligible for as many great opportunities as possible.

Drug Testing – An Engineering Co-op Perspective
by Bob Tillman
I'm spending a lot more time on drug testing now. Almost all of my field jobs now require random drug testing, and it doesn't happen when you first start, but it happens within a period of time at all of my municipalities. You can get pulled out for testing at any time because you're around heavy equipment. I had two of my best students come in and see me to tell me that they didn't want to interview at a place. One of them said to me, "Yeah, I have a lot of history in my hair."

Bob Tillman is a cooperative education faculty coordinator
in Civil Engineering at Northeastern University.

FINAL THOUGHTS ON INTERVIEWING

Remember, you can't control many aspects of interviewing. You can worry all you want about the quality of the interviewer or the caliber of the candidates who are competing for the job, but that won't change anything. Your goal should be to walk out of the interview feeling good because you did terrific research, employed a smart and thought-out strategy, answered questions honestly and enthusiastically, and asked provocative questions to wrap up the interview.

It's a terrific feeling to come out of an interview knowing you gave it your all. If, after that, another candidate gets the job because of superior experience, you really can't have any regrets—especially because your effort will pay off for you down the road, probably sooner rather than later.

We had a grad student working in co-op a few years ago who applied for a position as a co-op coordinator. In terms of experience, she was ninth out of the nine among the interviewees. This didn't faze her: She interviewed co-op employers, academic faculty, and students, formulated a great strategy, and wowed the five-person committee. Afterwards, she came down and told me, "That was great. Whatever happens, I did exactly what I set out to do."

Did she get the job? Not quite—she was runner-up to someone with more job experience. But within a month another position opened up in the department, and committee members *urged* her to apply and *recommended* her to the chairman of that committee. She used the same approach to ready herself for that interview and completely blew the competition off the map to get the job.

Lastly, give some serious consideration to doing a practice interview. At the very least, stop and think about what interview questions you hate answering, then see if you can practice them with your coordinator. Reviewing your strategy for a specific interview is something that most coordinators can do if a practice interview is not possible. The worst thing you can do is to assume that you have nothing left to learn about interviewing.

Chapter 3 Review Questions

1. If you were researching in preparation for an interview, what are two ways in which you can go beyond the job description to learn more about the job and the organization?

2. Which statement most appropriately captures how to approach an interview?

   A. Be able to summarize your strengths as an individual.
   B. More than anything, be sure to tell the interviewer what he or she hopes to hear.
   C. Try to just relax and be yourself—don't get too worked up about it.
   D. Try to make connections between your background and the job description.
   E. Be sure to give the interviewer plenty of personal background about yourself.

3. Think about the kind of job that you hope to get through your next search: For that job, how you would answer a question about your weaknesses?

4. What does the chapter describe as the most difficult type of interviewer for most interviewees?

   A. The Nonstop Talker
   B. The Silent But Deadly Interviewer
   C. The Olympic Judge
   D. The Big-Picture Person
   E. The Interrogator

5. Write a brief but effective thank-you note that would be appropriate to send to an interviewer as a follow-up step.

6. Name at least two great questions to ask at the end of any job interview.

CHAPTER FOUR
Keys To On-The-Job Success

By the time you have prepared your resume, gone on numerous interviews, and finally accepted a job offer from an employer, you may feel like it's time to kick back and relax and let the money come in from your job. However, nothing could be further from the truth: Accepting a job offer doesn't mean you've reached the end of all your hard work. All it means is that you've reached the end of the beginning.

When you have accepted a job, you need to start thinking about living up to your interview... and then some. In other words, anyone can walk into an interview and state that they are punctual, conscientious, hard-working, willing to learn, and happy to help out with some of the less glamorous tasks associated with a job. But it's very different to actually go out and live up to these statements all day, every day, for three months, six months, or longer.

Our goal in this chapter is to point out why your performance matters in your first professional job, and to help you get the best possible evaluation from your co-op employer or internship supervisor when it's time to go back to school. Some of the points we make here may seem like common sense, but we have learned that sense can be rather uncommon when it comes to some behaviors in the workplace. If you follow the guidelines in this chapter, you can prevent most co-op problems before they happen... which is infinitely easier than trying to fix something after it breaks.

WHY YOUR PERFORMANCE MATTERS

The best interns and co-op students realize that there is a great deal at stake when you're working in a job. An "outstanding" or "very good" evaluation from an employer means that:

- *You are a person of integrity who remembers your interview and delivers what you said you could deliver.* You come off as a hypocrite if you say that you are punctual, for example, and you start showing up late to work. Right away, the employer might start wondering what *else* might not be exactly true in what you said in your interview.

- *You are intelligent enough to realize that today's supervisor is tomorrow's reference.* Think about interviewing for a future job: It's nice to say "I'm an excellent worker with a great attitude," but it's highly effective and powerful to be able to say "I'm an excellent worker with a great attitude, and I would encourage you to contact my previous employer if you'd like to confirm this." Some employers may even call your previous employer without telling you: You don't want bad performance to come back and haunt you when seeking future employment.

- *If you are asked about a previous job in an interview, you want to be able to say in all honesty that you did a great job.* Interviewers can often tell how successful you were in a previous job by how you describe it. A common interview question is "If I were to ask your previous supervisor about what kind of employee you were, what would he or she say?" You have to be honest in these situations, and you want to be able to mention many positives.

- *You can feel good about yourself.* It's a lot more fun to do things well than to do things poorly. If you can complete your job with a sense of pride and accomplishment, you will have more confidence and will be better prepared for challenging jobs in the future.

- *You'll learn more.* The harder you work—the more you go "above and beyond" the basic requirements of the job, the more likely you are to learn more and gain valuable exposure to more sophisticated aspects of your field. That will give you a stronger resume and a better foundation for your future to go along with your excellent reference.

We realize that maintaining a strong work ethic and an excellent attitude can be challenging in some work environments. There may be situations in which you are asked to do work that is less fun, less interesting, and less educational than you had hoped. In fact, one unpleasant fact you have to accept is that almost *any* job you will ever have may require you to do some work that you don't enjoy. But if you can take on *all* work assignments with a pleasant and cooperative attitude, your employer will remember this and often will reward you with better assignments as well as an excellent evaluation.

UNCOMMON SENSE: WHAT IS AND ISN'T ACCEPTABLE IN THE WORKPLACE

As stated earlier, there are many aspects of work life that internship and co-op coordinators would *like* to believe are common sense: Things that everyone should know without being told. However, we have found that this is not always the case. As a result, here are some critical recommendations regarding how to avoid problems in the workplace. Some may appear obvious; others are less so. HOWEVER, no one should have to *tell* you these things once you have started your job. It is your responsibility to know these things ahead of time!

1. *You must be on time to work.*
After you have accepted your offer, be very clear about what time you are expected at work. Then make sure you are *always* there at least 15 minutes before that time.

When you become a co-op, intern, or full-time employee, you undergo a tremendous role reversal (see the following sidebar box). As a student, some people may be used to showing up late to classes. This is a bad habit, but you could argue that you're the customer: You have the right to not show up on time for classes. However, when an employer is paying *you* to arrive at a specific time and to work a specific number of hours, you do *not* have that right. Unless an employer specifically tells you that you can come in when you want to, you have to live by that employer's rules. For example, you can't just decide that you'll come in 30 minutes late and then eat your lunch at your desk instead of taking a 30-minute break at noontime.

From Student To Employee – An Engineering Co-op Perspective
by Bob Tillman
When you're a student, you pay the university for services in your role as a student. What are you paying for, and what do you expect to get out of it? How do you know that you're getting what you're paying for? What are the other amenities that you're paying for? It's a good exercise to think about that. Then I tell them that when you go out on co-op, *that role will exactly reverse itself.* You're being paid for your services now. So let's talk about some of the behaviors that don't work from your perspective as a student: Why do you think they would work as an employee as a part of an engineering team?

Students tend to connect with that pretty well. I want you to shift that role and almost forget that you're a student because it really will bring you down. For example, why do you have to show up on time? Well, if you don't, other work is not getting done; clients aren't getting billed. Let's talk about clients getting the bill, and what that means, as well as all the other people that fit into an engineering environment.

Bob Tillman is a cooperative education faculty coordinator
in Civil Engineering at Northeastern University.

Another point to remember is that too many interns and co-op students fail to leave any extra time in the morning to allow for possible traffic, parking problems, car trouble, or whatever. If it takes you 25 minutes to get to work, assuming that you catch every train or traffic light just right, then you probably should allow for at least 45 minutes to get to work. If you have to use this kind of excuse more than once over a six-month job, you need to change your habits: These excuses get old very quickly.

Lastly, remember one critical point: *Just because your co-workers arrive late, don't automatically assume that it's okay for you to do the same.* I recall one memorable student who had been given a warning by his employer because of repeated tardiness. His boss also told me that he sometimes came in by 9 but other times it was more like 10. When I talked to the co-op student about it, he thought that he was being unfairly singled out: "I see quite a few full-time people coming in at 10 or 10:30 every day!"

Co-op Job Success – A Student's Perspective
by Ted Schneider

- Meet as many people in your workplace as you can. And I do not mean this in only the superficial, "networking" type of way. If your co-workers are willing, do social things with them outside of work. I found that working closely with good friends on co-op was not at all distracting. I actually think that I performed much better when I worked for people who I liked and respected.

- An old one but still so true: Do not ever go to work late if you can help it. I knew people on co-op who were very good at what they did, but would fail to be promoted due to their tardiness. I also find that managers are much more flexible about giving time off if you are on time in the morning.

- Wear the right clothes. Wearing questionable or even semi-questionable attire makes you look like a fool. Enough said.

- Make sure to find a balance between asking for too much help and asking for too little. It's a difficult skill to master - I certainly haven't yet.

  Ted Schneider was an Accounting/MIS student at Northeastern University, Class of 2002.

When I looked into this, it turned out that my student was missing a few key facts: For one, he didn't know that these people were software developers. They had an understanding with management that they could come in late because they often stayed until 8:00 or 9:00 p.m. at night, well after my student left by 5:30! Secondly, the student had misinterpreted something his manager had told him when he was hired. When she said that it was possible to have a "flexible schedule," she meant that you could work from 7:30 to 4:30 with an hour for lunch, from 9 to 6 with an hour for lunch, etc. She did NOT mean that you could change your schedule every day, or that you could start your day later than 9:30. Lastly, I had to tell the student that sometimes policies are not always fair. Sure, the manager could have done a better job upfront about communicating the "unwritten rules" of that workplace, but she didn't. That simply means that the student needed to step up and be sure that his assumptions were correct.

2. *If being late or absent is absolutely unavoidable, give your employer as much advance notice as possible.*

There may be rare situations in which being late or absent is absolutely unavoidable. These primarily include car accidents, serious illnesses, or deaths in your immediate family. These things can't be avoided at times. However, you need to call your employer *before* the official workday begins. That may mean leaving a voice mail or answering machine message early in the morning before you show up: not in the late morning or afternoon, when everyone has already been wondering where you are for several hours. If you have a flat tire on the way to work, for example, you need to find the nearest possible phone so you can call in and give your estimated time of arrival. Always carry your supervisor's phone number in your wallet just in case something like this happens.

Unless you are completely incapacitated through illness or injury, YOU should be the one to call in: not your roommate, your mother, your roommate's boyfriend's sister's cousin or anyone else. And if you don't say how long you will need to be out, and you remain sick or otherwise unavailable the next day, you need to call your supervisor *again*.

3. *Keep personal phone calls to an absolute minimum.*

Working in an office with your own phone and phone number does not give you the right to have extended conversations with friends, family, and significant others throughout the workday. Beyond using your phone for business, you should generally use your phone only if you need to contact your co-op/internship coordinator, your physician, or to contact a family member in the event of an emergency.

One good way to avoid temptation is to not give your work number out to anyone besides your parents, your spouse or partner (if applicable), and your co-op coordinator. If you do need to make a five-minute phone call once or twice a week to arrange for plans after work, that probably would be acceptable in most workplaces. But generally you should avoid it whenever possible.

Over the last several years, cell phones have become incredibly common. As you have undoubtedly noticed, many people don't hesitate to use their cell phones in inappropriate places, including classrooms and—most incredibly in my opinion—restrooms. When you are working in a co-op job, your friends and family obviously will already know your cell phone number, and some people probably won't hesitate to call you during the workday. It's important to remember that making personal phone calls on your cell phone is really just as bad as making such calls through your company line. So unless you specifically need to use your cell phone for job-related purposes—which is not uncommon with PC support jobs, for example—you generally should turn off your cell phone before you walk in the door at work and keep it off until the end of the day. At most, you might check your messages during your lunch break.

Also, watch what you say over any type of phone while at work—even during your lunch break. Employers have accidentally overheard co-op students say the darndest things (e.g., "personal" comments from boyfriend to girlfriend or vice-versa) when the student/caller thinks no one is listening.

4. Use your computer for work-related activities only.

Like a telephone, a computer on your desk can be highly tempting to some interns, co-ops, and full-time employees. Most computers have at least some games (such as Minesweeper and Solitaire) on Windows, and more and more computers have Internet access, which can be an irresistible on-line temptation to some—especially those with e-mails accounts through AOL, Yahoo or Hotmail. More recently, AOL Instant Messenger (IM) and similar messaging systems are becoming widely available—many students are logged on to IM almost around the clock when they are in classes, so it's a habit that can be hard to break when you're starting a job. However, it's very important to do so—if you want to juggle your homework with e-mail and IM for hours on end, that's up to you. But when you're role has changed from student to employee, you're generally being paid to be at work, you shouldn't be using personal e-mail or IM on company time. You aren't being paid to chat with friends, after all. Even in an unpaid internship, this sends the wrong message to your co-workers and supervisor.

Unless your supervisor tells you that it's okay for you to practice exploring the Internet or World Wide Web as part of your job, you should avoid using it. If you really want the opportunity to play around on the Web, you could ask your supervisor if it would be okay to come in early or stay late in order to navigate the Internet or send e-mails with a clear conscience.

One student was fired from a co-op job last summer, primarily because this person used the Internet frequently and spent a great deal of time writing e-mail to friends during the work day. Try explaining that to a future employer. Other students have lost their jobs or at least hurt their evaluations by surfing the 'net or sending instant messages during work hours. After all, it's relatively easy for a computer network administrator to be able to see what applications anyone on the system has open, and it is completely legal and easy for organizations to monitor the e-mails that their employers send and receive to determine whether they are appropriate. Entertaining yourself on the computer during work hours certainly doesn't say very much about your initiative, drive, and judgment. Don't take chances—surf the 'net and use AOL IM at home or on campus!

Although this behavior is not excusable, these problems are most likely to arise when there is not enough work to do in a given job. Therefore, we will address that in point #5.

5. *If you don't have enough work to keep you busy, talk to your supervisor as soon as possible.*

If your supervisor needs to come around and see you playing a game, staring at the ceiling, or talking on the phone in order to find out that you don't have enough work, you have made a significant mistake. If you anticipate running out of work, try to give your supervisor as much notice as possible. It's perfectly fine to ask your supervisor what you should do if you run out of work: Especially if your supervisor isn't always readily available. Asking for more work when necessary shows that you are mature, that you take initiative, and that you have a good work ethic. All of these things reflect positively on you as an employee. Basically, *learn* from your work environment. Something ALWAYS needs to be done. Be proactive. Say something like, "I've finished 'X'; should I move onto 'Y'?" Your supervisor may be too busy to find a project for you and may be appreciative if you offer suggestions.

Many first-time professionals have begun a job with relatively low-level responsibilities but managed to end up with much more demanding jobs—simply by getting the easy stuff done quickly and correctly and then enthusiastically requesting more work to do.

6. *If you consistently have MORE work than you can do and do well, you should discuss this with your supervisor.*

Most good jobs will keep you very busy all day and all week. But if you find that you are working so hard that it is affecting the quality of your work, your health, and your enthusiasm for the job, you need to discuss this with your supervisor *before* it becomes a major problem.

Obviously, the best way to deal with this problem is to avoid these situations in the first place by using your interview to ask the appropriate questions about workload and expectations. But you can't always anticipate this problem. If talking to your supervisor doesn't improve the situation—or if you're unsure about whether you really are being asked to do more than what could be considered reasonable—call your co-op coordinator and get his or her input. Together, you can determine the best course of action.

7. *If you're confused or unsure about how to do one of your assigned tasks, say so. When you are assigned a task or given specific instructions, take careful notes so you won't have to request the same information again.*

The worst thing you can do if you're unsure about how to do a task is to just forge ahead and hope for the best. Usually, people are reluctant to ask questions because they are afraid of appearing stupid or ignorant. But remember: appearing ignorant is MUCH better than demonstrating your ignorance by doing your job poorly. Making mistakes on the job can be very costly to a company. Good employers expect you to ask for help when you need it to avoid these costly mistakes. Don't be afraid to ask a supervisor or co-worker to repeat or clarify instructions if you didn't understand the first time.

From Student To Employee – An Engineering Co-op Perspective
by Bob Tillman
I tell students that if you only learn two things when you go out on your first co-op, it's going to be a huge success: If you learn when to ask a question when you should, and when to keep your mouth shout when you should, you're really light years ahead. When you figure out, "This is a problem that I ought to be able to solve on my own" and know "What are the resources that are going to help me do it?" you're way ahead.

Another thing you learn out there is that there's a whole language out there that you haven't been exposed to, and you have to learn it. And the last thing is, "What are the other learning opportunities that are going on around you that aren't directly sitting on your desk?"

In engineering, if you can't do the routine work—checking calculations, adding numbers, checking drawings—you're never going to get more advanced work.
Bob Tillman is a cooperative education faculty coordinator
in Civil Engineering at Northeastern University.

A corresponding point relates to what you do with information or instructions when given to you. A smart employee shows up on the first day of work with a calendar for marking down due dates, deadlines, and meetings. A smart employee also brings a notebook and some writing materials so he or she can jot down specific instructions, guidelines, job requirements, computer procedures, and anything else you need to know. Nothing frustrates an employer more than a student who claims that he or she doesn't need to write things down, and then winds up making mistakes or sheepishly asking for the same information some time in the future.

8. Always keep your desk and/or work area reasonably neat and well organized.
This means keeping food and drink to a minimum in your work area. Keeping some mints or granola bars in your desk and a coffee cup on your desk is okay, but leaving food wrappers or food in plain sight at any time other than lunch is something to avoid.

Also try to keep items on your desk well organized. If asked to produce some paperwork, you shouldn't have to do a scavenger hunt in your desk or office to find it. If you're unsure about ways to organize your work materials efficiently, ask your co-workers for advice.

Co-op Job Success – A Student's Perspective
by Mark Moccia

In order to get the most out of your job, you must bring a strong work ethic to the table. Once your employer sees you are willing to work hard, they will be impressed. Then, after you have shown the ability to work hard, you can polish your "working smart" skills: By this I mean getting things done quickly AND more efficiently for the company/department.

It is also important to learn the preferences/personality of your boss immediately. It is important to know whether your boss is the type that wants assignments done in five minutes or 30 minutes. A question I still ask to this day is, "When do you want this done by?" This avoids any confusion as to when you are supposed to finish an assignment and also avoids potential conflicts.

Speaking of conflicts, if you encounter one at work then it is important to alert your immediate supervisor. While fellow co-op students might lend an ear to your problems, they might not always have the best solution because they are just as inexperienced as you. If the conflict is with your supervisor, bring it to the attention of your co-op advisor quickly. I have heard stories of co-op students who feel invincible because they are only on assignment for three or six months and imagine that the company cannot fire them because it would look bad for the company. This could not be further from the truth; if you have direct conflicts with your supervisor or are not performing to your potential, you can be fired just as easily as a full-time employee. I encourage co-op students to use their best judgment in these situations and avoid "blow-ups" at all costs. If you can do this, work hard, and bring a positive contribution to your time on the job, a good reference and evaluation will follow.

Mark Moccia was an Accounting/MIS student at Northeastern University, Class of 2002.

9. Always use good judgment regarding attire and hygiene in the workplace.

You need to convey a professional image every single day that you are employed. The standards may differ from one workplace to another: Some places allow casual attire, for example. But be careful in how you interpret dress codes. Casual attire generally still means that you should wear a collared shirt and nice pants: not blue jeans or shorts. Sometimes you get away with dressy black sneakers, but not always white sneakers. Women should avoid low-cut blouses, halter tops and tank tops. Open-toed shoes or sandals are a bad idea, too. You should always wear clothing that is clean, wrinkle-free, and without any holes in it. For men in casual environments, you should still shave each day. It's not a bad idea to look at how your co-workers dress, but you want to err on the conservative side—don't assume it's okay to dress a certain way just because one or two co-workers choose to wear extremely informal attire at work!

Another point here: You may think nothing of wearing an eyebrow ring or a nose ring or a tongue stud, but an employer may find these items to be unprofessional. Save your unusual jewelry for after-hours and weekends.

Co-op Job Success – An Employer's Perspective
by Steve Sim
There are two things to keep in mind when coming for an internship/co-op at Microsoft:
1. *Know your limitations.* This is a fact at MS. There will always be someone who knows more about business, technology, marketing; etc. than you here (especially technology). Knowing your limitations also makes you aware of how these people can help in your development.

2. *Don't be afraid to fail.* You're here to learn about how we do things. MS is a place where we do things, if anything, for the right to learn how to do that thing better. You'll always be challenged to do something right the first time, and possibly, you do it right the first time. Or did you? Have you tried <u>everything</u> possible? Who's to know that better than you?
Steve Sim is a Technical Recruiter at the Microsoft Corporation.

---

10. Don't misunderstand the meaning of the words "casual work environment."

As stated above, you may be able to wear more comfortable and informal clothing in some work settings. But don't think that "a casual work environment" means that *everything* is casual. Just because the company president wears jeans and jokes around with you when he or she visits your desk or cubicle, it doesn't mean that it's okay for *you* to pop into his office and joke around with him or her. Likewise, a casual work setting is not a place where work is done in a casual, laid-back manner. In fact, there are many very intense organizations that allow casual attire. Remember, casual work environments are just like all other jobs in one important way: You still can get a poor evaluation or get fired by not living up to your interview and by not living up to the company's expectations and standards.

Another point about casual environments: It is *never* acceptable to wear headphones in any workplace unless your boss specifically *suggests* it. This is true regardless even if you are working on your own, doing boring, monotonous work. Wearing headphones on a job sends a clear message that you're not really paying attention to what you're doing and that you don't care if you look unprofessional. Even if co-workers wear headphones, don't make the same mistake.

11. When asked to do something that you don't enjoy, do so without complaining or sulking.

I visited one employer who was Director of MIS for a prestigious organization in Cambridge. He mentioned that a co-op student from another university (not Northeastern, thankfully) complained when he was told to do a fairly monotonous and time-consuming task with the computer system. The employer told me, "The thing that I asked him to do is something that *I* have to do pretty often, and I'm the Director of the whole department! And he tells me that *he* shouldn't have to do it?"

There's a valuable lesson here: Sometimes students are quick to assume that they are given boring tasks to do because they are "only students." As we saw in this example, this can be an erroneous assumption at times. Sometimes, you may be asked to do something simply because it has to get done, and it doesn't matter who does it. Employers appreciate *any* employee who does routine, unglamorous, necessary tasks without complaining, whining, or sulking.

If an employer asks you if you enjoy doing a certain task, be honest but be pleasant about it. If you don't like doing a given task, you might say, "Well I don't mind doing it, but it's not my favorite part of the job..." Be ready to point out some other tasks that you would be excited about doing.

12. Go above and beyond your basic duties.

One reason some students fail to get great job evaluations is because they basically show up at 9, do their job in a competent, acceptable way, and go home as soon as possible. If you want to get a very good evaluation, you need to go beyond this. You need to be willing to put in extra hours if necessary. You need to show some pride and excitement in what you do: If you're asked to do something, give them even more than they expect in terms of effort, ideas, and attitude. Always think about ways in which you could do your job more efficiently, whether it involves helping your supervisor, your co-workers, or just the tasks you do on your own. The following sidebar box is a great example of this phenomenon.

Above and Beyond – An Arts & Sciences Co-op Perspective
by Ronnie Porter

We had this co-op job that on paper didn't look very exciting. It was doing some computer work for a company that manufactured an instrument that allowed anaesthesiologists to know if a patient undergoing surgery was getting to a level of wakefulness. So there was a lot of data entry—looking at the data, reviewing the data, etc.

What this person ended up doing was taking this information and learning a tremendous amount about what kinds of drugs were used on what kinds of patients for what kinds of surgeries. He really came to understand the sleep patterns and how all that interrelated. He actually had so many conversations with his co-workers that he got to go to an open-heart surgery and witness an eight-hour surgery along with the person who was teaching the anaesthesiologist how to use this device. He came back and said, "You need to rewrite this job description! It's the most exciting position, and there are so many things you can learn in this job. I didn't really realize that, looking on the surface."

Ronnie Porter is a cooperative education faculty coordinator
in Biology at Northeastern University.

---

13. Understand what an employer's expectations are regarding time off from work.

Before you begin any job, you should make sure you have total clarity regarding your start date and end date as well as time off from work. In many cases, co-ops and interns—or full-time hires for their first six months on the job—have NO vacation time coming to them! So don't assume that it's going to be fine to take a Spring Break if it falls in the middle of your work term; don't imagine that there will be no problem if you want to take a week off in the middle of the summer.

What days do you get to take off? Any days that are official holidays for your employer (i.e., Memorial Day, Labor Day). Technically, that's all that an employer is required to allow you to take. But can there be exceptions to this? Sometimes, yes, but you shouldn't count on it. For example, a student who works in a position that is far away from his or her home may *ask* his or her employer if it would be okay to conclude a work assignment prior to Christmas rather than going home and coming back for three or four days before the assignment technically ends. The employer may or may not grant this request.

What can you do to improve your chances of having a request for unpaid time off granted? Do the following:

- *Keep such requests to an absolute minimum.* If you know you're going to ask for time off after Christmas, for example, don't press your luck by looking for additional time off earlier in the work period.

- *Only ask if you have an excellent reason for requesting time off.* Besides Christmas and other religious holidays, it may be reasonable to ask for a day off to attend an out-of-state wedding, for example. Or if you've been working 12 hours a day for a month during tax season in an accounting job, it may be reasonable to ask for a day off when things slow down once again. Generally, though, you don't want to ask unless it's an absolute necessity. You never know when you might *really* need the time off.

- *Do such an outstanding job during the work period that your employer will be willing to give you time off.* An outstanding worker definitely has a much better chance of having requests for time off granted when necessary. In some cases, an employer even raises the subject to offer a reward to an extremely productive worker.

Look at it this way: If a worker has a bad attitude, is late or absent frequently, does mediocre work, and constantly needs to be supervised, an employer is bound to look at a request for time off as the final insult.

14. Keep your internship or co-op coordinator informed about any major problems, dilemmas, or unpleasant situations that arise.

The majority of students will not have any major problems arise during their work experiences. However, there is always the possibility that you might face problems that are beyond what we expect you to handle without our help. Please call your coordinator as soon as possible if you are:

- *the victim of sexual harassment or other abusive behavior from your co-workers or supervisor.*

- *laid off from your job, regardless of the cause (i.e., budget cuts, buyouts).*

- *given a warning about being fired.*

- *fired.*

- *being paid less than promised.*

- *having problems with your supervisor that are difficult to discuss.*

Additionally, call your coordinator if you have brought up any of the following problems with your supervisor, and the conversation has not produced a change:

- *You are given far too much or too little work to do on a regular basis.*

- *Your job is not what you were led to believe it would be, and you are not having a good learning experience.*

- *You are stressed out due to the work, your co-workers, or your customers.*

Sometimes a problem can be easily fixed if addressed quickly, while it can become a huge issue if ignored. When in doubt about the seriousness of a problem, contact your coordinator.

Co-op Job Success – A Student's Perspective
by Gabriel Glasscock
Don't sit back and say to yourself "I'm just an intern." This is your job, and you have the ability to make the most of it. Some jobs will have downtime; it's just a fact. You can spend that time surfing espn.com, and boston.com, or you can go to your boss and say "Hey, I have some downtime, is there anything I can do?" In one such situation, I went to my boss, and she ended up shipping me off to a very expensive class on Web development in which I learned an immense amount, and thus had more responsibility at work.

If there is a problem at the job, don't be afraid to talk to your manager. If you're not doing anything stated on your job description, don't go silently. Remember: it's up to you to take charge. Your advisor or boss can't do anything unless they know about it.
Gabriel Glasscock was an MIS student at Northeastern University, Class of 2002

---

15. When faced with ethical dilemmas, make sure that you always act in a way that allows you to maintain your self-respect, integrity, and clean record.

We hope that you won't face too many ethical dilemmas during your practice-oriented work experience. However, any job that you will ever have potentially can present you with tough situations. For example, would you cheat on your timesheet: even if you were sure you could get away with it? Sadly, I have had students caught for falsifying their hours, and they were terminated immediately—all those potential references and resume-building experiences permanently ruined or severely damaged, just for the possibility of a little extra money.

What would you do if you became aware that another employee was stealing money, supplies, or equipment from the organization? If you make a potentially critical mistake and become aware of it later, should you tell your supervisor or simply hope that no one notices your error?

Ultimately, every individual has to decide for himself or herself how to act in situations when no one—not your coordinator, your supervisor, or your parents—is looking over your shoulder. Basically, it's simple: Do the right thing, and you will save yourself a lot of guilt, fear, and worry about the consequences. If you're not sure about what the right thing is in a given situation, contact your coordinator.

16. Sit down with your manager during the first week of your job to set goals for your co-op work period.

If your program uses a standard work evaluation, you and your manager should review the entire evaluation upfront to know how you will be judged at the end of the work period. Additionally, though—whether or not your program requires it—you should write at least three goals for your work assignment, and you should do this in the first few weeks of your work experience.

What might your goals be for a given work assignment? They could vary dramatically depending on your major, the job, and your level of previous experience. For some first-time student employees, one goal may simply be to learn how a corporation works and how to perform effectively day-in, day-out for six months in a professional environment. Some goals may relate to refining soft skills, such as improving presentation skills, proving to be a dependable employee by arriving at work early every day, or perhaps learning how to multitask or to prioritize in the face of deadlines or multiple responsibilities. Other goals may be more advanced and/or more geared to specific job skills: "I hope to find out if I'm comfortable working hands-on with patients of all backgrounds as an aspiring physical therapist;" "I intend to learn how to use ASP to make database-linked dynamic websites," or "I want to be immersed in the activities of this cat hospital so I can learn if this veterinary environment is right for me." With goals in place, you and your manager will have a better mutual understanding of what you are supposed to be accomplishing in your role, and you can both do a better job of tracking your progress toward these objectives as the work period progresses.

Setting Goals – A Health Sciences Co-op Perspective
by Rose Dimarco
First I would suggest that within the first couple of weeks that you sit down with your boss and talk about expectations to nail down what people expect of you and what you can get out of the position. Always remember that this is typically a paid position, so it's value added that you bring to the employer.

Obviously there will be learning opportunities for you but not at the expense of what you were hired to do. I think a pitfall is when there is some conflict or misunderstanding that you don't bring up with an employer—or an employer doesn't bring up with you—and then it manifests itself and causes tremendous problems with that relationship.

Rose Dimarco is a cooperative education faculty coordinator
in Physical Therapy at Northeastern University.

---

17. Do everything you can to become part of the work team and not "just a student."

To make the most of your job experience, make an effort to integrate yourself as fully as possible in the workplace. This is especially important if you work at a company that employs more than one student. Some students have the tendency to go to lunch with their fellow students, socialize outside of work only with fellow students, and generally avoid significant contact with full-time employees. This is understandable—in a new and strange situation, a person may be tempted to cling to something or someone who is familiar or similar. However, if you fail to make some connections with full-time employees, you're missing out on one of the great things that co-ops, internships, and other practice-oriented roles have to offer.

Initially, talking to these people will help you learn the "unwritten rules" of that particular workplace regarding what is and is not acceptable and appropriate. Ultimately, your experience can become a chance to rub elbows with people who work professionally in your field as well as other areas of possible future professional interest. Simply joining these people for lunch or for a bite to eat after work, you may pick up invaluable information about:

- how to succeed in your job.

- whether or not you have much in common with people who work professionally in the career that interests you.

- what kinds of coursework, job experiences, or self-study projects will help prepare you for a great career after graduation.

- how people perceive the pros and cons of their own career choices.

Another benefit of getting to know full-time employees is that they will be more likely to think of you as part of their group or team, and therefore more likely to give you tasks to do that are appropriate to your interests, experiences, and skill levels.

Becoming Part of the Work Team
by Marie Sacino

Our computer information systems interns at the Queens Public Library work on the client side, providing 24/7 functionality, troubleshooting, changing hard drives, and ghosting as ongoing support tasks. Interns also work in the field on new PC rollout projects—2,000 new PC installations at branches throughout Queens this past summer.

What does it take to be a successful IT intern? Philip Darsan, Director of Information Technology at Queens Public Library, has some good thoughts. "An intern needs to begin to understand their working environment, to ask more questions, to utilize the department's organizational chart, to be cognizant of naming conventions—firewalls, deployment, DNS, IP," Darsan says. "We need serious students who really want to learn and don't watch the clock. Most IT personnel work 50 to 60 hours a week.

"I try to give the students an opportunity to open their eyes to the technology," adds Darsan. "Just how wide they choose to open them is up to the student. I'm interested in students who have a technician's perspective and who are customer-service oriented. I'll ask a student, 'How well do you communicate?' Without solid communication skills—interpersonal, reading, writing, speaking—there will be little growth for a technical support person."

Marie Sacino is an Associate Professor of Cooperative Education at LaGuardia Community College

---

18. However, be careful about mixing business and pleasure.

Sure, you want to be part of the work team. This can mean going out for lunch with co-workers or going out after work. It's great to fit in and be part of the gang, but you need to be careful when it comes to drinking with co-workers or getting romantically or sexually involved with people at work.

First, let's talk about alcohol. In some organizations, drinking is very much a part of the culture—you may be encouraged to drink at lunchtime before going back to work for the afternoon. In some offices, going out for beers after work is routine—or even having beer or wine brought into the office on a Friday afternoon by the organization itself! What should you do? You have to decide for yourself, but remember a few things. If you're underage to drink in your state, it's simply a bad idea to drink with co-workers—even if they urge you to do so. I had a student years ago who got fired from a prestigious firm because he drank at an office Christmas party. His boss had been proactive—telling him in advance that he could come but he could not drink. At the party itself, though, co-workers twisted his arm and got drinks for him: His boss found out, and he was fired.

Even if you are legal to drink and enjoy doing so, you should be discreet about doing so. I would never recommend that you take the initiative in ordering a drink if you're out with a colleague. If you're with several people who are drinking, it might not be a big deal to have a beer or a glass of wine—but be very moderate at most.

The same goes with getting physically involved with people at work. In particular, it's never advisable to date a supervisor or someone who works for you. Even if someone is a fellow intern or a co-worker of similar age, you need to proceed with caution. What will you do if you break up with someone, and then you need to keep working closely together? Not a fun situation for either party. At the minimum, the best bet is to wait until after you complete your job before considering any relationship with a co-worker. Remember, also, that making unwanted advances can lead to embarrassing disciplinary issues as well.

One other reminder: When are student employees most likely to forget that it's not such a great idea to get involved with co-workers? You guessed it: When they've been out drinking at lunch or after work! If you're not careful, this issue can be double trouble, and it can affect how people perceive your professionalism at work.

19. If you're on a full-time job, your job performance should be your highest priority.

When you're in classes full-time, that should be your top priority. But when you're on co-op or on a full-time internship, you need to focus the bulk of your energy on performing your co-op job to the best of your ability.

Two factors can interfere with your job performance if you're not careful: First, some students choose to take classes while on co-op or an internship with long hours. To do so, you may need the permission of your co-op employer and your co-op or internship coordinator. Before seeking their permission, however, be honest with yourself: Can you take on one or two classes without jeopardizing your job performance or your academic performance? If in doubt, it is best to avoid taking classes on co-op or to keep them at an absolute minimum.

Another situation may arise for seniors: Naturally, seniors are concerned with getting full-time jobs after graduation. Sometimes, seniors may be interviewing for full-time jobs and co-op jobs simultaneously. However, once you've started a co-op job, you should keep any full-time interviewing to an absolute minimum. To go on one or two interviews through your Department of Career Services during your co-op job—with your co-op employer's permission, and with the understanding that you will make up for the missed hours—may be acceptable. To miss significant time from work to go on numerous interviews is not acceptable. For that matter, it's not that smart: Many seniors get full-time job offers from their last co-op employers IF they are outstanding performers. Don't jeopardize your co-op job—and a possible future offer—by looking elsewhere for full-time jobs during your work term.

20. If you're working part-time while attending classes full-time, you need to manage your time very effectively.

There are a few possibilities here. Some students regularly juggle an internship with full-time classes. Likewise, some full-time co-ops opt to stay with their co-op employer on a part-time basis when their co-op experience officially ends. Either way, working part-time poses several challenges. I have had some full-time co-op superstars who absolutely destroyed their reputation with their employer because of their failure to adapt to being a part-time employee.

Here are a few tips to avoid this pitfall:

- *Don't over-commit.* Some students ambitiously promise to work 25-30 hours per week part-time. The employer counts on this resource, only to have the student start to realize that it's too much to balance—so he cuts back to 18 hours…. Then 15. This is all very annoying to the manager. Better to under-promise and over-deliver—don't commit to more than roughly 15 hours of part-time work per week while in full-time classes unless you really, really know you can handle it.

- *Set a regular schedule and stick to it as much as possible.* Committing to 15 hours a week generally doesn't mean that you go in whenever you feel like it in a given week. Look at your course schedule and block out some times that you can regularly do. Maybe one whole day and a couple of half-days; maybe two whole days—it doesn't really matter as long as your supervisor is comfortable with the arrangement and you generally stick to it. If you have voice mail and e-mail at work, make sure to include a message that informs everyone about your hours and what to do in your absence. Likewise, if you have a desk, office, or cubicle of your own, prominently post your part-time schedule so people will know when you will be working next. In scheduling, also remember that coming in for just an hour or two here and there seldom works well.

- *Plan ahead.* As soon as you get your syllabi, note the dates of exams and major due dates on your calendar. Maybe you have a week in which you have three midterms. In that case, you can approach your boss with plenty of notice to let her know that you'll need to be out for a few days. There is really no excuse for calling in the morning to say that you can't come in because you have an exam that day.

Effective Internships – An Arts & Sciences Co-op Perspective
by Ronnie Porter
I think in addition to the skill sets, there's a professionalization/socialization piece that doesn't occur as much when you're working on a part-time basis, ten hours a week, as opposed to doing it full-time when you're a member of a team and equally counted on.

I think the important thing is that at the outset you really set some goals for the time period of the job. I think that's really critical in any situation—that students have goals and that employers agree as to what those goals are. I think it's even more critical when you're there on a limited basis—when you're going to have to pick and choose what you do or what you want to learn and still have that coincide with what's needed at the organization. Otherwise, anything could happen. Things might turn out okay, but in other situations they might turn out to be very disappointing with people feeling like they've wasted their time.

Ronnie Porter is a cooperative education faculty
coordinator in Biology at Northeastern University.

21. If you are relocating for a job, be careful about how your situation can affect your perceptions of the job.

If you take advantage of an opportunity elsewhere in the country, you may end up living with other students who work for the same employer or with a different employer. As a result, students sometimes end up comparing notes about jobs, employers, supervisors, co-workers, etc. If both students are having a good experience, this is fine. But if one student is having a bad experience, everyone in that living situation needs to make sure that they continue thinking for themselves. In other words, decide for yourself whether or not you are having a good experience: Don't let anyone tell you what you should or shouldn't be thinking about your unique situation. This is true of any roommates who live together while working, but the negative effects can be magnified when you're living a long way from home and perhaps eating, breathing, and sleeping your practice-oriented experience every minute of the day. It's a powerful experience, so you have to make sure you maintain some objectivity.

Working in a different part of the country can be an excellent idea. In a sense, you're guaranteed of having a "double learning experience"—you'll learn on the job, and you'll learn off the job about what it's like to live in a different region. At best, you may find a place you enjoy more than your home city. At worst, you'll appreciate your own region, campus or home more when you return.

22. Return to school with a network of new contacts.

Lastly, don't miss the golden opportunity of co-ops and internships: When you're working in any position, make sure that you have acquired a network of new contacts before you complete the job! You have the opportunity to earn the respect of many people in your field during your work period. That's great, but make sure you capitalize on that by collecting business cards and/or contact information before you leave. You never know who might be in a position to help you out when you're networking for another job in the future. If you only know one or two people at your worksite, you might be out of luck if those people move on and can't be located.

Assuming you've done all you can to make a positive impression, having plenty of names can pay incredible dividends in the future when it comes time for another job search. Even if those individuals can't directly hire you, they may be in a position to recommend you for other jobs or to give you valuable career advice. Don't miss the boat!

Networking – An Engineering Co-op Perspective
by Bob Tillman
Who did you network with? Can you tell me ten new people who you know now, who know you? People who you could talk to down the road about a job? Because if you didn't, you wasted your time. That was the freebie out there. That's the value added that you don't get someplace else.

Bob Tillman is a cooperative education faculty coordinator
in Civil Engineering at Northeastern University.

THE EMPLOYER'S PERSPECTIVE

All of the recommendations listed in this chapter generally reflect the expectations of most managers and organizations. HOWEVER, remember: *Every manager and organization is different.* One of the most important survival and success skills in any job for the rest of your career is to pay close attention to the written and unwritten rules of each workplace. Don't make assumptions about what is or is not okay!

Find out what drives your supervisor crazy and what makes her happy, then make any adjustments accordingly. Some bosses really don't care what time you arrive as long as you do a great job—others are upset if their employees don't arrive *early* every day! In some environments, wearing jeans and a t-shirt is acceptable; in others, wearing anything other than business formalwear is a major mistake. In some organizations, how you dress, speak, and act may have very different rules depending on the department. I visited a small software company in Cambridge a few years ago: The software developers wore ripped jeans and t-shirts and were playing chess at 2:00 in the afternoon. Meanwhile, the marketing personnel were wearing suits and working hard from 9-5 with a brief lunch break, while the accounting personnel were wearing business casual clothes and working fairly flexible hours. All of this was happening in a company of about 40 people. Any co-op student entering that environment would have to be very careful in figuring out what was and was not appropriate behavior.

Regardless of your position, you must begin to think and act like a professional. Professionals remain on the job until a project is completed in a timely accurate manner.

Don't worry whether you are being compensated or not for extra work. A marketing manager recently calculated what his salary worked out to be on an hourly rate, only to discover that he was making just a few more dollars per hour than his co-op students!

On-The-Job Performance – An Employer's Perspective
by Mike Naclerio
Students can get the most out of their jobs by taking the initiative. Many co-op positions in the business field have heavy administrative functions built into them. Do the administrative part thoroughly and without resentment and find additional opportunities to contribute in the organization. Do not get stuck in the gossip and pity trap of how bad my co-op and/or supervisor is. It is all what you make of it. Ask for more work and if your supervisor doesn't have anything, come back to them with a proposal to fix a major problem they may be facing or overlooking. Do not wait for the company to provide you with the opportunity because many organizations are just too busy to focus. If you come to them with a well thought out plan that addresses a key problem, you are sure to stand out.

As far as dealing with conflict, just deal with it. If you are having a problem with a supervisor or co-worker, ask them if they have a few minutes to talk, go somewhere private and clear the air. There is no time for drama in the workplace and most people should respect the directness.

Mike Naclerio is the Director of Relationship Management at the workplace HELPLINE.

SPECIAL CONSIDERATIONS FOR HEALTH SCIENCE PROFESSIONALS

If you're majoring in one of the health sciences—nursing, physical therapy, occupational therapy, pharmacy, athletic training, cardiopulmonary science are some examples—you may do clinical assignments as well as co-op jobs. In both cases, you're working in the world of practice as opposed to the classroom. However, there are some key differences between the two experiences. The following sidebar box addresses them. As you'll see, the contrast can be ironic— some behaviors that are extremely appropriate for a health sciences co-op can be quite out of place on a clinical!

Clinical Versus Co-op – A Health Sciences Co-op Perspective
by Rose Dimarco
Clinical affiliations in the health care professions are a place in the world of work where students have to demonstrate clinical skills that they've learned in the classroom as well as some professional behaviors that are appropriate for that level of student. There is a curriculum; there are objectives that the student must fulfill in the out-of-classroom experience. They are graded on it, and they are supervised by someone from the university—typically in all the health-care professions. Co-op is driven by a job description: Opportunities for learning are there in co-op, but they're not the first thing.

In most cases, clinicals are assigned—there's no interview. But approaching it? Well, I'll tell you a quick story. One of my better students on co-op came back and said, "I'm having a hell of a time on my clinical." And I said, "Abby, how can that be? You just shine in everything you touch." And she said, "Rose, I don't know how to delegate. As a licensed therapist, I have to demonstrate that I know how to delegate to appropriate personnel, and I do it all! As a co-op, I was delegated to, and I don't know how to get out of my own way! So if I need towels, I go get them. If I see a linen closet that needs organizing, I organize it. I make time for it—I stay after work. My clinical advisor at site would say, "Abby! That's what you should have given the aide to do!"

So that transition is more of a challenge than anything—getting out of that mindset. So a clinical is more student objective-centered, based on a curriculum.

Rose Dimarco is a cooperative education faculty coordinator
in Physical Therapy at Northeastern University.

FINAL THOUGHTS REGARDING ON-THE-JOB SUCCESS

Getting on top of the many details in this chapter obviously has an enormous impact on the job experience. For better or worse, professional jobs are always about *momentum*. If you start off the job doing all the little things right and avoiding any pitfalls mentioned in this chapter, the employer starts believing in you. You may get more and better responsibilities as a result. However, momentum also can work in reverse! If you have trouble getting to work on time, if you gripe about doing your job, if you are given low-level tasks and do them poorly, then there is a negative domino effect. You probably would start getting less work and less responsibility. If something goes wrong with one of your assignments, you're more likely to be blamed for it—fairly OR unfairly.

By adhering to the principles discussed in this chapter, you will avoid unpleasant conversations with your supervisor and coordinator and build a foundation of success in the workplace that will help you get your next job and excel in it. Above all, if in doubt about what to do and how to do it, ask someone. Then you'll find out how to live up to your interview.

Chapter 4 Review Questions

1. List three different ways in which performing well on your job or internship will benefit you.

2. Depending on traffic or public transportation issues, let's say that it could take you anywhere from 30 to 50 minutes to get to work. If you absolutely have to be at work by 8:30 a.m., what time should you leave?

3. Give three examples of specific goals that you would like to be able to set for your next internship, co-op job, or full-time job.

4. Name four on-the-job situations in which it would be highly advisable to contact your internship or co-op coordinator.

5. Describe three common mistakes students make when trying to juggle a part-time job or internship with full-time coursework.

CHAPTER FIVE
Making Sense of Your Experience

Eventually, your job will end, and you will return to the classroom. Whether your experience was terrific, terrible, or anywhere in between, it would be a missed opportunity to just put it behind you when you return to the classroom. At this point, you need to take the final steps toward getting credit for your co-op as well as figuring out what comes next in your career. At Northeastern, this process includes a) turning in an evaluation and b) completing a reflection requirement.

Receiving an evaluation and fulfilling reflection requirements offer you a chance to make sense of what happened while you were on co-op. Because the primary goal of co-op is to learn from anything you experienced at work—whether positive or negative—the evaluation and reflection processes will help you gain some perspective on how you did and what you can take away from the experience. This will help build self-awareness—including a sense of what you need to do to keep growing and improving as a professional in the future. It's not uncommon for a student to emerge from a co-op or internship with a greater sense of urgency about the classroom. For that matter, it's not unusual for students to improve dramatically in their coursework after co-op. In addition to seeing the practical relevance of the material in the "real world," taking classes sometimes feels pretty easy after a demanding work experience!

As the following sidebar box indicates, internships and co-op jobs don't only answer some career questions that you may have—they also may raise new questions regarding about what comes next.

Returning To The Classroom – An Arts and Sciences Co-op Perspective
by Ronnie Porter

In my program, students sometimes realize what the theories really meant when they were put into the practice—or sometimes the other way around: They've done things on co-op and then studied the theory and figured out why things were done a certain way. Either way, it just naturally flows into the academics and into thinking about how they want to do things next time around on their co-op.

Through their co-op experience, they may know that they need to take courses to enhance their expertise in a certain area. In Arts and Sciences, the question should not be, say, "Can you give me a list of all the philosophy jobs?" We say, "That's not the right question." We're interested in "Why are you interested in philosophy and what do you want to do with it?" So it's a different approach. There's no list of jobs, rather there are a lot of conversations around what the person wants to do and what their hopes and expectations are about how they're going to use this information that they're learning.

Ronnie Porter is a cooperative education faculty
coordinator in Biology at Northeastern University.

YOUR EVALUATION

As your co-op job comes to a close, you generally will receive an evaluation. Most programs have a standard form that employers can complete and return to the program coordinator. Often you will be asked to summarize the job and your sense of how it was as an experience, while your supervisor will write up her or his thoughts on your responsibilities, strengths, areas for further professional development, and on your soft skills: interpersonal relationships, dependability, judgment, etc. You also may be given an overall rating, such as outstanding, very good, average, marginal, or unsatisfactory.

Some employers will give you an evaluation form that is typically used for all employees in their organization. These forms can be several pages long and are quite detailed. At some organizations, the format involves asking you and your manager to reflect briefly in writing on how successful you were in reaching your job-related tasks and objectives.

Whatever your evaluation looks like, keep a few things in mind when receiving your first performance evaluation:

1. *Don't take it too personally.* You and your manager may not see eye to eye on how you did in your job—and it won't always because your supervisor has a higher opinion of your performance than you do! You may receive criticism that you believe to be inaccurate or unfair. Regardless, you want to end your relationship with any employer in a gracious, classy manner—don't blow it because of an impulsive, emotional reaction to evaluation comments.

2. *View the evaluation experience as a learning opportunity.* If you have communicated consistently with your manager throughout your co-op, you should not be too surprised by your evaluation. In any event, your evaluation gives you things to think about and talk about with your co-op coordinator—it can lead to specific goals for personal improvement and success in your next co-op. No one is perfect, and no one is perfectly self-aware of all of her or his strengths and areas requiring further development. Use the evaluation as a tool in your professional development.

3. *If you feel your evaluation is unjust or unfair, take the initiative to discuss it with your coordinator.* Getting evaluated on co-op is hardly an exact science. Some employers may rate students higher than they deserve because they fear that a negative or neutral review will cause undesirable conflict or impair your academic progress. Other employers may have impossibly high standards or just believe that most employees should receive average reviews unless something really astonishing was accomplished. In other situations, you may have a change of manager midway through your co-op, or perhaps you reported to numerous people or maybe even to no one at all. Obviously, any of these developments will affect the fairness or accuracy of your review.

Discuss any of these concerns with your coordinator. We know that these things happen, and it also can be quite challenging for us to figure out the truth amidst many different perceptions. Your coordinator should be able to provide you with a more objective and balanced view of how you did if you're not sure what to think about your review.

4. *After a few months have gone by, review your evaluation again.* It's easy to lose your objectivity when you're working somewhere 40 hours per week. After you have been out of that specific work environment for a good while, you may find that it's easier for you to consider the positives and negatives of your review more openly and less emotionally. It's also good to reconsider your performance before you begin your next job search, so that you are ready to discuss how your job went with a future employer. This is a good opportunity to show self-awareness and graciousness. Even if you have lingering bad feelings about a previous job or supervisor, you need to move on and take the high road when discussing past events with a potential new boss.

While most co-op students get anxious about their initial performance evaluation, the great majority of our students at Northeastern University do very well in the eyes of employers. Probably at least 90 percent receive "very good" or "outstanding" evaluations. Still, everyone always has ways in which they can improve, and it's generally very helpful to get feedback from an experienced manager in the professional world.

PURPOSES OF REFLECTION

As co-op, internships, and other forms of practice-oriented education become a bigger piece of the learning puzzle at many colleges and universities, more schools are beginning to require some form of reflection requirement for students returning to school following co-op. Why do co-op programs require reflection? There are numerous reasons:

1. *Making connections between classroom and the world of practice.* One purpose of co-ops and internships is to give students a practice-oriented element to their educations, making learning "hands-on" instead of just learning about theories. Reflection often requires you to think about how a work experience brought classroom concepts to life, or how practical work experience changed an understanding of something you *thought* you understood in a course. In return, your job experience gives you raw material that you bring with you to class to help you understand new concepts and theories in your field.

Integrating Practice With Coursework – A Health Sciences Co-op Perspective
by Rose Dimarco
I find that as an undergrad student in health care, you learn quickly when to do something and how to do it. The why you are doing it—why you are doing that range of motion or stretching exercise or providing certain pharmaceutical drugs—comes in the classroom. So it's up to you to take the where and when and connect it with the why. Now you're slowly going to evolve from studying nursing to becoming a nurse—that's going to come from that interchange.

Rose Dimarco is a cooperative education faculty coordinator
in Physical Therapy at Northeastern University.

---

2. *Having an opportunity to compare your experience with those of others.* Going to reflection seminars gives you a chance to hear about where your classmates worked, what they did, and how it all went. It can be useful to hear about how others dealt with challenges that they faced and to hear the thoughts that upperclassmen have about the job experiences after going through the process repeatedly. At best, you may be able to learn from the successes and mistakes of others.

3. *Learning about future job options.* Hearing about other students' experiences may give you some added perspective about where you might want to work in the future as well as jobs or organizations that you may wish to avoid. HOWEVER—Be careful about drawing conclusions from the experiences of others! Just because one industrial engineering student complains bitterly about her internship at Amalgamated Suitcases, does that mean that YOU wouldn't like the same job? Maybe, maybe not. In the same reflection seminar, you may hear another engineering student praising his supply chain

management job at an organization called advancedlogistics.com—does that mean this job is great for everyone? Of course not.

Exploring Job Options – An Engineering Co-op Perspective
by Bob Tillman
The discussion now is going to be, "Tell me more about what you're looking for the next time. Are you looking for more of the same but just at a higher level? Is it a new challenge? A career exploration you're looking for? Skill development? Are there certain projects you want to work on? What's the itch? Let's identify that.
Bob Tillman is a cooperative education faculty coordinator in Civil Engineering at Northeastern University.

Whenever I start my reflection seminars, I usually tell the tale of two students who did the exact same job at the same time with the same employer. In one reflection seminar, the first student said, "My PC support job was fantastic—I'd recommend it to anyone. The day goes by really quickly because there's always something new to handle—you're not stuck behind a desk; you're going all over the company to troubleshoot problems. When you go see end users, they're usually upset about their computer problems, but when you fix the problem, they are SO grateful! What a great job!"

At the next reflection seminar, that student's co-worker complained bitterly about his job: "Don't ever work in PC support! What a bunch of headaches—you come in and try to get a project done, and you keep getting interrupted constantly by end users. They're generally pretty clueless about computers, and they're in a foul mood when you go to see them. Every day I went home with a headache."

Which student is "right"? Both... and neither. The quality of a job experience is very much in the eye of the beholder. When students describe their previous jobs, listen more carefully to their descriptions of the job duties and the reasons why they liked or disliked their jobs. Make up your own mind as to whether that job would be good for you.

4. *Having the opportunity for more detached and objective appraisal of one's experience, after the fact.* Working at an organization full-time is kind of like being in an intense relationship. Whether you're in a romantic relationship, living with a roommate, or working in a job, it can be easy to lose your perspective when you're immersed in the situation. Positively or negatively, you might do things you wouldn't ordinarily do—and then wonder why that happened, after the fact.

Reflection gives you an opportunity to make sense of your experience in a more detached, open way, after you are no longer in the situation. This may lead to new insights and a new appreciation of what it all meant.

141

Reflection also can be quite surprising for both students and coordinators. One time I was running a reflection seminar for entrepreneurship/small business management students. One student reported that he had worked at a small restaurant but found it frustrating because the entrepreneur was highly secretive about the financial affairs of the business. "My guess is that he didn't want to show me the books because he was cheating on his taxes," the student said. "But I guess that's what you have to do to make it as an entrepreneur."

I managed to hold my tongue and asked if anyone else in the room had another perspective on the situation. A second student raised his hand, "My family has run a business for several generations, and my grandfather *went to jail* for basically thinking the same thing as your boss." It was a powerful moment and a great chance for the group to reflect on the challenges and ethical dilemmas that entrepreneurs face—as well as considering the potential consequences of running a business that is engaged in illegal activity.

FORMS OF REFLECTION

Generally, there are many ways in which you can fulfill your reflection requirement. Which one will you end up doing? It depends partly on what works best for you and partly on what your coordinator finds most advisable given your circumstances. All reflection methods have pros and cons, so let's consider briefly the different forms of reflection.

1. *Small-group seminars*: Most Northeastern students participate in a reflection seminar in a small group—usually no more than 15 students. For the time being, business students are required to go to one 60-minute session with their coordinator and a group of students in their field. On the positive side, this method is fairly quick and painless for most students and coordinators. It also gives students a chance to exchange ideas and experiences with classmates. On the negative side, it's hard to go into serious issues in great depth in a one-time, one-hour session. Also, some students may feel awkward or uncomfortable sharing their job experiences—especially if something unpleasant happened at work. For these students, another reflection method may be preferable.

2. *Writing a reflection paper and/or keeping a journal:* This is another common form of reflection. Your coordinator may provide you with some questions or topics that can be addressed in a paper. Often the focus is not so much on a plot summary of your work experience: instead, the idea usually is to try to make connections between the real world and the classroom and to get across what you learned about yourself and the organizational world while on an internship or co-op—even if that included getting fired from your job! Some students even write weekly journals reflecting on their development through the job experience—it can be quite remarkable to look back at a list of your anxieties and concerns before day one at the end of a six-month full-time

co-op. Here are some questions that might be considered for a paper or journal:

- How has this job experience helped you understand concepts that you previously learned when taking classes in your major? Has this experience changed your attitude toward being in classes and your ability to perform since returning to campus after completing your job? How have liberal arts classes helped you build useful transferable skills for the professional world?

- What was the purpose of your job? How did your job fit into the overall organizational mission?

- How did you learn how to do your job? Formal training? Personal instruction by your supervisor? "Peer-to-peer" learning—did you pick things up from co-workers? Figuring things out for yourself? Break down the various ways you learned about appropriate behaviors as well as work tasks or products.

- What differentiates an excellent manager or supervisor from a poor or average one?

- How and why did your job confirm or change your career direction?

- Describe the organizational culture of where you worked and whether or not this culture is the best for you as a worker.

- What were the norms or "unwritten rules" regarding what was and was not acceptable where you worked? Was it difficult to learn these norms and adjust to them?

- How would you rate the quality of your job as a learning experience?

- What did you learn in this job that had nothing to do with your technical skills or your major/concentration?

- How would you rate your performance in the job, regardless of the job's quality?

- Now that you have had this experience, what are your plans for your next job, whether co-op, internship, clinical, or post-graduate?

Journals and papers are advantageous in that they provide a chance to really go into depth about what you learned, and they also are a more private form of reflection. The downside is that they are more time-consuming and don't allow you the chance to hear the perspectives of fellow students.

3. *Reflecting via e-mail, online message boards, and the Web.* Some coordinators may set up electronic ways of helping you reflect on the job while you are still working. You may have questions e-mailed to you for your consideration and response. Sometimes online message boards or the Web are used in order to create places where students can connect with other students

and their coordinator despite being far away from campus. The best thing about these methods is that they help you have opportunities to reflect when there is still time to make changes in your performance or address problem areas at work. The negatives include the time involved and the risk of information getting into the hands of those who are not meant to see it. Additionally, the technology is a hurdle for some co-op programs.

4. *Taking a work-related class DURING your co-op.*
   In the last few years, some Northeastern students have had the opportunity to take a one-credit course during their co-op. The students who took this course on ethics in the workplace were allowed to have this count toward completing their reflection requirement. The class generally meets only a few times in the early evening, though there are also online assignments and discussions. In addition to getting reflection credit for this course, many students found this to be a great opportunity to discuss ethical issues or concerns while they were in the midst of them in the workplace.

5. *Having a one-on-one meeting with your coordinator.* Occasionally—most often in special circumstances—a coordinator may find it acceptable to meet one-on-one with a student to complete the reflection requirement. This is not typical, as it is a very labor-intensive method for a coordinator who may have over 100 students returning to classes after co-op. If something particularly difficult happened on the job, though, this may be an important and useful option in order to confront problems, learn from mistakes, or to determine if the coordinator has issues that must be addressed with the employer.

GETTING CREDIT FOR YOUR WORK EXPERIENCE

For most students, getting an at least average evaluation and completing a reflection requirement means that they will get a passing grade for their work experience. (Most co-ops and internships are graded on a pass/fail basis, if at all.) Sometimes, though, the outcome is in doubt. Any of the following can jeopardize your ability to get a passing grade for your work experience:

- failing to notify your coordinator about your job before it begins

- accepting an offer from one employer, only to go back on your agreement to accept an offer with another employer

- quitting a job without getting your coordinator's permission first

- getting fired (or getting a poor evaluation)

- failing to turn in an evaluation in a timely manner

- failing to complete a reflection requirement within two months of returning to school

In the end, your coordinator will determine the grade you receive for your work experience. Make sure you understand the grading criteria. Make sure that you're never in a borderline category by doing a great job and completing all steps with your coordinator! After all, failing your work experience doesn't look so great to future employers who will be reviewing your transcript.

FINAL THOUGHTS ON CO-OP SURVIVAL AND SUCCESS

After reading this much of the guidebook, you should have a good foundation when it comes to understanding workplace survival and success. If you can apply the concepts that we've covered in these pages, you will emerge with greater self-awareness, a sense of accomplishment, and a set of experiences that will entice employers looking to hire new graduates. You also will have a new appreciation for how, why, and where learning happens as you go from one job to the next as well as from the classroom to the world of experience.

For a co-op coordinator, internship director, or career services professional, the most satisfying part of the job is seeing students come in with retail stores and restaurants on their resumes and graduate as professionals with a keen sense of who they are, what they want, and what they are capable of accomplishing through hard work. I have seen students who were barely able to get a low-level administrative job on the first co-op who ultimately graduated with incredible experience and a very attractive job offer. I often tell students that internships and co-op jobs are not sprints: They are marathons that reward those who display persistence and consistent effort over the months of a co-op position.

But perhaps I should let some of our top Northeastern University students tell their stories to give you a better sense of what I mean.

Making Sense of Your Co-op – A Student's Perspective
by Ted Schneider

There is nothing like co-op for turning inexperienced freshmen into successful professionals. The constant transition between class and work is painful, tiring, and repetitive but also extremely exciting, rewarding, and invaluable. After four co-op positions in four terrifically different locations, I "know" that I have had a college experience that cannot be matched by experiences had by those at traditional universities.

When I go home for the holidays, I laugh about my high school friends' nervous questions regarding the interview process. Since freshman year, I have had approximately 25 interviews for "professional positions." Interviewing has become such a commonality for my peers and myself that most of us look forward to it almost as if it is a fun challenge - not to see if we could do well, but to find out if we could do even better than the last time. NU students—or co-op students anywhere I guess—are so far ahead of their traditional-program counterparts when it comes to professionalism that we have a reason to be a little proud.

Ted Schneider was an Accounting/MIS student at Northeastern University, Class of 2002.

Here's another one:

Making Sense of Your Co-op – A Student's Perspective
by Mark Moccia

To be honest, I did not know what to expect from co-op. I heard mostly positives about co-op. However, I was still unsure of how I was going to be treated, the relationships I would have with management, how much work I would receive, and other job-related concerns. The most surprising thing I learned about co-op is that you are, in fact, treated just as a full-time employee. You are expected to work standard hours (and overtime if needed), take your job seriously (and not as a temporary assignment where you can "goof off" for 3-6 months) and contribute in a positive manner. The co-op program is the main reason I attended Northeastern: I would have been making a $100,000 blunder by not getting the most out of co-op. The other amazing advantage of co-op is that if you perform well enough, you have the inside track on a full-time position with the company!

I have always been a great student. However, the co-op program has made me realize that it takes more than excellent grades to be successful. Co-op has taught me that you need to have good transferable skills, such as communication, multi-tasking, time management, and the ability to interact with all levels of the organization. Working with corporations has taught me to take my focus on schoolwork and apply it to the business world, specifically through the co-op program. Without the co-op program, my grades would be just as strong but I would not have the skills and savvy to match it.

Mark Moccia was an Accounting/MIS student at Northeastern University, Class of 2002

Here's one more!

Making Sense Of Co-op – A Student's Perspective
by Gabriel Glasscock

When I began my co-op career, my expectations weren't high. I expected to be exposed to the corporate climate and have minimal responsibilities at a few companies, graduating with my foot in the door at a few places. Before I knew it, I was in Tampa, Florida, standing in a classroom in front of 80 over-analytical recent college graduates, giving them lectures on the Java programming language. The most surprising thing I've learned is that you can ride this co-op roller coaster as fast as you want to if you're not afraid to take on challenges.

Co-op has humbled me but also made me aware of my capabilities. It tests your resilience, and helps you realize what you really want to do with the rest of your life. It has helped me mature and exposed me to many things. I now know what it's like to have 12 friends laid off on the same day!

Co-op prepares you mentally for the reality of working and dealing with life after college. I truly consider myself lucky to have had these opportunities. In some areas, I consider myself 100% different, and for the better. Typical four-year programs? Heck no! CO-OP!

Gabriel Glasscock was an MIS student at Northeastern University, Class of 2002.

The rest of the book features appendices that may or may not be useful to you right now. Appendix A covers the job search process through the Co-op Learning Model. Appendix B details how to write cover letters—whether for obtaining an internship, a co-op job or your first job after graduation. Generally, you won't need to write a cover letter if you're applying for a job through a co-op or internship program, but sooner or later you will want to learn how to write a cover letter that is every bit as strategic as the interviewing approach described earlier in the book. Appendix C features some handouts that I like to use in my Introduction to Co-op course. Some may be useful in helping to fine-tune your resume or interview, while others are thought-provoking scenarios that can be the good basis for written reflection or in-class discussion.

Good luck with your co-op career, and remember: The goal is to shine and not simply survive!

Chapter 5 Review Questions

1. Why do many students start getting better grades in classes after completing a co-op or internship?

2. What are three benefits of attending reflection seminars?

3. Think about the last job that you held. What was the *purpose* of that job? How did it fit into the goals of the organization that employed you?

4. Name three situations that could result in a student not getting credit for a co-op or internship.

5. From the three lengthy student sidebar boxes on the benefits of co-op, which one resonated the most with you? Why?

APPENDIX A
The Co-op/Internship Process

In this book we have covered a great deal of information about co-op. Nonetheless, you may very well be wondering "what do I do next?" Every program has its own rules, regulations, and idiosyncrasies, causing difficulty in making generalizations about the job search process across universities. However, there are enough commonalities to make it worth our while to review them here. More than anything, though, I want to make sure to preface this information with a warning: *The job search process is always evolving and changing over time. Universities are continually revising the job search process, making changes to computer systems and student requirements such as deadlines for turning in resumes, creating e-portfolios, and changing ways to get referred to employers.* **As such, ALWAYS stay in touch with your coordinator to be sure of the requirements and deadlines for your specific program!** If in doubt about when you need to get started, make contact and find out sooner rather than later. Failing to do so could make all the difference between success and failure in your job search.

CO-OP LEARNING MODEL

The Co-op Learning Model is a simple but useful way to understand the three primary phases of the co-op process: preparation; activity; and reflection.

The Preparation Phase
The preparation phase includes all of the activities that you undertake to get ready for your co-op or internship. Contrary to the opinion of a few misinformed students, most programs are not job placement services. In other words, you can't just waltz into your coordinator's office a few weeks before your scheduled work period begins and—just like that—get "assigned" to a job. The system doesn't work that way. Why not? The most important reason is that we want you

149

to own the responsibility of your job search, so you will understand how to do everything you need to do to get a job for the rest of your professional career! Therefore, we don't write your resume for you, we don't tell companies who to hire, and we require an employer evaluation to help us determine if you get a passing grade for your work experience.

Because of all of this, preparation takes time! Generally, you will be asked to revise your resume more than once, and some students may go on more than a dozen interviews before getting and accepting an offer.

The Activity Phase
After you get a job, you start working regularly with your employer; the work period is the activity phase. During this phase, your focus should be on understanding and meeting your supervisor's expectations regarding everything from work hours to job responsibilities, setting goals together to ensure that you have a mutual understanding about your level of job performance.

During this phase, it also may be advisable to check in with your coordinator back at school—especially if any concerns or problems arise. The objective is to return to school with the best possible evaluation and reference.

The Reflection Phase
After you return to classes, you need to complete the reflection phase to get credit for your co-op. Basically, though, you will need to make sure that your coordinator receives your evaluation and find out if any reflection requirement needs to be fulfilled. It's also advisable to update your resume soon, while the job is still fresh in your mind.

Now that you have an overview of the co-op process, let's take a closer look at the details that may be involved in each step.

WORKING WITH YOUR INTERNSHIP/CO-OP COORDINATOR

As mentioned briefly in Chapter 1, it's critical to build a good working relationship with your co-op coordinator—and with other co-op faculty if necessary. Here are some key pointers:

Stay On Your Coordinator's Radar Screen. Given that your co-op coordinator works with hundreds of students each year, you can't expect him or her to hold your hand through the process. It's absolutely critical that you take responsibility for finding out and remembering how early and often you need to come in and what you need to accomplish each step along the way. If you're not sure, call or send an e-mail. "I just didn't have time to get in touch" just doesn't cut it with us—not when it takes all of one or two minutes to update us with an e-mail or voice mail at whatever hour of the day or night. If you're not in touch with us regularly—especially during the months before you're scheduled to start your job—we have to assume that you're really not that interested in working.

Know How To Determine Your Co-op Coordinator's Availability.
Find out if your co-op coordinator can be seen individually either by appointment or by going to walk-in hours. But how can you find out when a given co-op coordinator is available? See if your coordinator has a calendar—either online or just outside the door of their offices.

If you have trouble finding a time to meet with your coordinator, you should drop an e-mail or call your coordinator to see if additional times are available. If we don't know that you're trying to meet us, we can't help to accommodate you!

Here are a few other helpful hints about working with co-op and internship coordinators as well as career services professionals. With a little thought and communication, you can avoid considerable frustration.

1. *If you are on a tight schedule in general, try to schedule appointments.* Some students have limited free time available due to classes, part-time jobs, clubs, and varsity sports. If you fit this description, you need to be proactive, scheduling appointments ahead of time and asking your coordinator for ways to ensure regular meetings. Most coordinators and career professionals will schedule meetings at irregular times if a student has legitimate conflicts and is proactive and polite about addressing the situation.

2. *If you prefer to come to walk-in hours, try to come first thing in the morning and/or bring homework or reading material if you must come when it's busy.* During the months leading up to the beginning of a work period, coordinators can be very busy seeing students. Some students end up frustrated because they haven't really thought about how to avoid the walk-in logjam. There are many ways to minimize your waiting time. First, come in early—early in the day and early in the process. Many college students are not early risers, so most coordinators tend to have shorter walk-in lines during the morning hours. Anytime after 11:30 tends to get really busy during the peak times of year. Likewise, if you come in several months before your co-op for that first resume review, you will beat the rush and be in good shape the rest of the way.

   Sometimes, though, you can't avoid a long wait—especially during peak months. With this in mind, bring some homework or reading material—that way you won't sit around feeling impatient if you do need to wait a while.

3. *If you really can't come in every week or so during referral period, you really need to stay in contact via e-mail or voice mail.* Some students keep popping by during a busy afternoon walk-in hour time... only to find that there is a long line. If they get discouraged and leave, the coordinator has no idea that the student has made any effort to get in touch. Thus, you really need to stay in touch by voice mail or e-mail—even if it's just to give a quick update regarding

your job search or to let your coordinator know that you're having difficulty coming in during the available times. If you fail to let us know that you're having a problem, then we won't know!

4. *Be reasonable about what you expect your coordinator to be able to do for you in person, on the phone, or by e-mail.* In person, don't expect your coordinator to write or rewrite your resume for you or to describe numerous available jobs to you. You need to do many things for yourself. As for e-mails, bear in mind that they should not replace individual meetings. One of my frustrations is when students e-mail their resume to me and ask me to critique it or correct it. It's incredibly time-consuming to edit a resume this way, as it results in extremely long e-mail replies: "On the fourth line of your second job description, three-quarters of the way across the line, add a comma before the word 'demonstrated'" Ugh! There may be situations in which long e-mails are unavoidable—for example, when you are facing a major problem at work and can't openly talk about it on the phone or come in to the office because you're on the job full-time—but resume reviews are generally not one of those situations. Many situations just require a personal meeting.

5. *When faced with frustration or uncertainty, assume the best of your coordinator.* If your coordinator doesn't reply to your call or e-mail as quickly as you like, assume the best in this situation. It may be because you wrote your e-mail on Monday night, and the coordinator was out visiting companies on Tuesday. Then that coordinator may be welcomed back to the office with a few dozen e-mails, 15-20 voice mails, and a long line of students filling up the whole morning of walk-in hours. It doesn't mean that you have been forgotten or that your coordinator doesn't care. If more than three days go by without hearing back—or sooner if you are facing a real emergency—follow up politely and professionally: "I'm sure you're very busy right now.... I just wanted to follow up to make sure you got my message and to see if there was anything else I should be doing right now. It would be great to hear from you when you get a moment. Thanks!"

This is good practice for when similar situations arise with managers and co-workers on co-op. In either situation, this kind of message goes a long way in terms of getting a quick and professional response.

THE STEP-BY-STEP PROCESS

Preparation Phase

Step 1 – Become Aware of ALL Deadlines and Requirements As Soon As Possible.
If you're a first-time student—and especially if you are a transfer student, meet with your coordinator as soon as possible to learn about your options regarding when to start co-op. *Don't assume that you can start your co-op or internship*

whenever you feel like it! Co-ops and internships are not guaranteed for all students—if you blow off meeting with your coordinator, the consequences generally will be severe. If you miss deadlines, you may not be allowed to use the resources of the co-op department in finding a job. The student who does this will end up seeking his or her own job and risks getting a failing grade for co-op.

Step 2 – Have a One-on-One Meeting With Your Co-op Coordinator.
This is a mandatory step in most programs. You will identify and discuss your short-term and long-term co-op and career objectives with your coordinator. You also will bring a hard copy of your resume to your co-op coordinator, so he or she can critique and edit it. Save these edits, and use them to revise your resume accordingly. Bring a hard copy of your revised resume to your coordinator along with the edits, so your resume can be proofread quickly and effectively. It may take a few rounds of corrections, but eventually your coordinator may ask for an electronic copy of the finalized resume to e-mail to employers.

Step 3 – Review Co-op Job Descriptions And Rank Them.
Once your finalized resume has been approved by your co-op coordinator, you generally will be allowed to start pursuing jobs. Make sure you understand your school's system—including any computerized job listings.

Study the description and requirements and try to determine which jobs represent good learning experiences for you as well as being within your reach. If you're not sure, ask your coordinator. Many coordinators will require you to print out job descriptions that are of great interest to you—this will help you and your coordinator to determine if the job is a good fit and if you meet the qualifications. Keep the job descriptions in a folder.

Step 4 – Meet With Your Co-op Coordinator to Review Your Job Rankings.
The next step generally is to review your job rankings in an individual meeting with your co-op coordinator. Find out how early you can do this, and also if there is a deadline for making this happen. Bring your folder of printed job descriptions to your co-op coordinator.

Your co-op coordinator will review your rankings. In all probability, he or she will have additional suggestions and also may determine that a given job might be too much of a reach for you. Don't be discouraged—it's part of the process, and sometimes seeing your "reach" jobs can help your co-op coordinator suggest other jobs that are steps in the direction of your "reach" jobs. In many but not all programs, coordinators will limit how many jobs you can pursue simultaneously. Coordinators definitely do not want students to just fling dozens of resumes at employers—they want you to be more selective. This also means that you should really know each job description when you come in: Don't just look at a company name or job title and print out the job description without really thinking about how you match up with the job duties and requirements.

I can tell you that students vary *dramatically* in how they interact with a coordinator. I have had students interrupt a meeting with another student—or a phone call—by walking into my office regardless and saying "Send this to Gillette for me for the such-and-such job." Such behavior says a great deal about a student's professionalism—it's never a good idea to treat a coordinator as if she or he is your servant or administrative assistant.

On the other hand, there have been any number of times when I have been absolutely wowed by a student. If someone comes in and is upbeat, professional, and polite, I'm going to try that much harder to help them. There have been many occasions when such a student came in asking about a job that was already filled—and I was so impressed by them that I encouraged them to apply for other good jobs... and even recommended them to an employer!

Step 5 – Stay in touch with your coordinator regularly throughout the process. After your rankings and referrals have been completed, your resume will start going out to employers. Most coordinators e-mail resumes out at least once per week. At this point, there are many different possibilities. Some students get a few interviews out of their first batch of resumes to go out to employers; others don't get any—especially less experienced students.

If you get an interview, let your coordinator know—even if only by e-mail or voice mail. Ask your coordinator how often you should check in. At some point, your coordinator may be able to fill you in a little. You may be told that a company has not contacted any candidates yet, or you may learn that you are not one of the candidates chosen for an interview. In any case, your coordinator will suggest sooner or later that you select some more jobs and then come in again to discuss the new selections.

The worst thing you can do is to get discouraged by not getting interviews or by getting interviews and no offers. These developments don't always come easily! Some students start on time and do everything right—but then disappear completely after they send a batch of resumes and get no reply! Other students definitely intend to stay on top of things, but then they get distracted by mid-terms or other academic responsibilities. *You have to stay in touch*—even if it's just to say that you haven't received any calls and aren't sure what to do next.

Repeat the process of ranking jobs, getting referrals, and going on interviews as many times as you need to in order to get a job. In a job search, you never know if you're ten percent of the way to getting a job or whether you're incredibly close. But you always have to assume that you're really close and that with another push of effort it will happen for you.

Step 6 – Responding To A Job Offer.
Remember these key points:

- Unless you are in a dire financial situation, money should not be the deciding factor in which job you accept. Money is NOT a motivator! That's been proven in many studies. What WILL motivate you? A job with the following characteristics:

  —You like the work itself
  —You have opportunities for growth and advancement
  —You have opportunities for achievement and recognition

  If you're choosing between a great learning experience that is an unpaid internship, or a mediocre experience that pays $8/hour, which will you choose? Depending on your field and other alternatives, you very well may be better off taking the unpaid position. On the other hand, there's nothing wrong with taking a great job that pays $14/hour over a comparable job that pays $10/hour.

  For most students, my advice is to go after the best learning experience at this point in your career. If you focus on your career development now, the financial rewards will come sooner or later—and you'll be happier in the meantime going to work every day.

- If you are offered a job which is not your first choice, you can ask the employer for a short time to consider the offer—no more than three business days. Chapter 3 details how to put an offer on hold gracefully.

- Once you have accepted a job, meet with your coordinator to do an agreement form and any other paperwork. **As of January 2003, it is absolutely critical that international students (here on F-1 and J-1 visas) receive work authorization BEFORE starting ANY job in the United States.** After 9/11, the government has become incredibly strict about international students who are working without formal authorization. Deportation is becoming much more common. For all students, though, meeting with your coordinator is a good opportunity to discuss success factors for your co-op job, including how to avoid problems and get the possible evaluation and reference.

- REMEMBER—do NOT accept a job unless you are prepared to honor your commitment no matter what else happens. It is completely unacceptable to renege on your acceptance if you get another offer later—even if the other offer is a much better offer for significantly more money. Students who don't honor their agreements risk getting a failing grade for co-op. If in doubt, ALWAYS talk to your coordinator before you accept a job offer.

- Re-read Chapter 4 of this guidebook before starting your job, as this chapter has many good ideas about on-the-job success.

Developing Your Own Job
Chapter 1 goes over the guidelines for developing your own job, so you should re-read them if you have any questions about how the process works.

Most importantly, remember that students developing their own jobs still need to be in regular contact with their coordinators. You can't go off and do a job without getting it approved beforehand by your coordinator.

Activity Phase

You are expected to complete the entire work period once you have accepted a job. In other words, you can't do a job for a few weeks and then decide you don't like it and just quit. There may be rare occurrences in which a student may be released from their commitment—for example, if the employer misled the student about the nature of the job, or if harassment is going on. HOWEVER, it is the student's responsibility to bring any problems or concerns to the attention of the co-op coordinator instead of just quitting as soon as a problem arises. Send an e-mail, make a call—anything—just let the co-op or internship coordinator know what's going on and get her or his advice before taking action.

Note that most co-ops and interns rarely get vacation days during their co-op work period: There is no "Spring Break" for students working winter and spring, for example. Likewise, students can't end a full-time co-op job in early December to get an extra long Christmas break: At best, your co-op will end a few days before Christmas. Likewise, students working winter/spring may end their co-op on a Friday and start classes by the following Wednesday!

You are expected to work on any days that the organization is open—meaning that some students will get a day off on Columbus Day, while others will not. Organizations have different policies regarding paying students for holidays, but most often employers simply pay you for whatever hours you work.

Contact your coordinator with any problems that arise on the job.

Reflection Phase

Most of the whys and wherefores regarding reflection can be reviewed in Chapter 5. To get credit for co-op or an internship, most programs require that you:

- complete your co-op job successfully

- turn in a relatively good evaluation form

- complete a reflection requirement or some other follow-up activity

APPENDIX B
Writing Effective Cover Letters

If you're looking for a co-op job with the assistance of a co-op program, you may not need to write any cover letters. It may be enough to submit your resume through a co-op coordinator in order to obtain a job interview. Sooner or later, though, you will need to write an effective cover letter in response to a job listing. I have read thousands of cover letters over the years, and it never fails to amaze me how bad they can be—and how good they can be.

The most common mistake made by job applicants is to write a cover letter that really doesn't say anything useful. The bad cover letter will be extremely short, often saying no more than this:

"In response to your listing (in The Boston Globe, on monster.com , etc.) I am writing to be considered for the position of Accounts Payable Coordinator (or Financial Analyst or Desktop Support Manager). As you can see on the enclosed resume, I have a degree in business. I am a hard-working individual who would be a good fit for a company in any number of different accounting and finance roles.

"I am excited about the possibility of working for your organization. If you wish to arrange an interview, please contact me at...".

What's wrong with this approach? It breaks the cardinal rule of cover letters: **You need to think of the cover letter as a bridge connecting your resume to a specific job description.** Far too often, job seekers take the easy way out: They write a simple cover letter that is so general that it can be modified quickly to send to another employer. While this has the advantages of being efficient and convenient, there is no question that this is a short-sighted perspective. When a recruiter or manager reads through dozens of cover letters, inevitably he or she sees quite a few that are just like this. Fairly or unfairly, the reader of the quick and general cover letter will make several assumptions about the candidate. It's easy to conclude that the applicant is probably flinging his resume at dozens of jobs—maybe even sending out a hundred cover letters and resumes in the hopes of getting a small handful of interviews. The potential interviewer has to question whether the applicant has even given any serious consideration to whether he really wants the job in question. It's certainly hard to believe that the candidate really wants this specific job, and why would you ever want to hire someone who doesn't really want the job at hand—even if they have a terrific resume?

On the other hand, a great cover letter will not get you a job—but it can get you in the door for an interview, even if you're not a perfect candidate on paper. At best, the cover letter can make the interview much easier by covering the fundamental, strategic reasons why you are a good match for the job. So let's take a look at what comprises an effective cover letter before walking through some specific examples.

ELEMENTS OF AN EFFECTIVE COVER LETTER

Yes, writing a cover letter is more time-consuming than you might like because of the need to tailor each letter individually for each job that you're pursuing. The good news is that there are numerous elements that can be applied to *all* cover letters. While you can never reduce cover letter writing to a formula, you'll find that they become easier to write because the style issues are quite consistent. Here they are:

Start off with a flush-left heading that gives the appropriate name, job title and address of the cover letter's recipient. Usually this would look something like this:

Ms. Lenora Fritillary, Human Resources Manager
Schlobotnick Products
123 American Way
Roanoke, VA 33547

You then would begin your cover letter with "Dear Ms. Fritillary,".

At other times, you may not have a name and may have to use a job title:

Network Adminstrator
Byte Size Products
1200 Easy Street
Walla Walla, WA 94239

In this situation, you will have to start your cover letter with the more formal "To Whom It May Concern." That's a little formal, but if the job listing offers no contact name, you have to go with it. If the job is one that you are pursuing without any contact name, you can call up the main number of the organization and ask for the name of the person who is in charge of marketing, human resources, or information systems. It's always better to have a real live person listed as the cover letter's recipient unless the ad obviously indicates that the employer prefers to avoid a personal contact.

Briefly state how you learned of the job opportunity (if there is one) or simply express your interest in potential employment. Just as you always want to target a specific individual when you write your cover letter, you definitely want to write a cover letter with a specific job description in mind whenever possible. Otherwise, you face the challenge of writing a cover letter that implies that you're equally excited about any of a wide range of possible jobs. That's a much tougher sell.

Here are a few ways in which you might describe how you learned about the job at hand:

Example 1:
I am writing to express my interest in the Accounts Payable Assistant position, which was advertised in last Sunday's *Boston Globe*.

Example 2:
Speaking to my friend Patti O' Furnichure, who works in sales at your organization, I learned that your organization is looking for a market research analyst.

Example 3:
In response to your listing on monster.com, I am writing to express my interest in the Human Resources Assistant position.

If you have no choice but to submit a cover letter without knowing what jobs might be available, you are forced to write something more general.

Example 1:
I am writing to express my interest in working for your organization. Given that your company is known for their work in financial services, I was wondering if there would be a suitable position available for a finance student with excellent organizational skills and a great academic background in the principles of finance. I have strong analytical skills and would be effective in working in positions involving mutual funds, stocks, and bonds.

Example 2:
After doing extensive research on the Internet, I know that your company has 600 employees at your Dedham office. With this in mind, I was wondering if there might be opportunities available in PC/LAN support, database

administration, or web development. I am a quick learner with computers, and I have the flexibility to be effective in any number of IT functions.

Make several strong connections between your resume and the job description at hand whenever possible. At this point, you need to put your resume next to the job description and read the two side by side. Are there specific job requirements that you definitely have? Why would this employer hire you instead of someone else for this job? Why *wouldn't* this employer hire you? Making these assessments will help you figure out what your strategy should be—for the cover letter as well as for a potential interview. You need to come up with three or four concrete reasons as to why you are excellent candidate to interview.

REMEMBER—the goal is to do more than justify why you thought it was okay to submit your resume! Some cover letters come off as a little defensive or apologetic in this way: "Your job description said that you were looking for someone with an accounting degree who also has strong knowledge of advanced functions in Excel. I hope to receive my accounting degree by the end of 2004. While my knowledge of Excel is not advanced, I am certainly very willing to learn..." If you're writing many sentences like these, you probably just aren't a good enough match to merit consideration.

Another common mistake—both in cover letters and interviews—is to talk too much about why the job would be great for you—rather than why you would be great for the job! This ill-fated applicant might write something like this: "Working for your organization would give me a great opportunity to build my knowledge of human resource management. I would be very excited about enhancing my computer skills in this position as well...." Showing enthusiasm about the job is always a good idea, but not if you're only excited about what the job will do for you. You have to imagine yourself as the person reading a big pile of cover letters and resumes—your goal is to find the person who can best help in your organization in this role: not to find the candidate who most needs your help! As such, the hiring manager is going to pick out some number (probably somewhere between three and ten) of candidates who appear to be the most plausible for the job, based on the cover letter and resume.

We'll consider some full-fledged job descriptions and resumes shortly. In the meantime, here are a few examples of ways in which a good cover letter might make connections between a resume and a job description:

Example 1:
Your job description details the need for candidates to have a strong background in marketing as well as excellent communication skills. I received a grade of A- in my Introduction to Marketing class; in particular, I earned a top grade on an analysis of market segmentation in the automobile industry. Additionally, I have worked in numerous retail positions, honing my customer-service skills and refining my knowledge of merchandising. As for my communication skills, I have obtained considerable presentation experience in my business classes and have

augmented this by taking an elective in Public Speaking—a course in which I performed extremely well.

Example 2:
From your ad on monster.com, I know that you are seeking a highly trustworthy individual with a solid understanding of accounting principles and Excel for your Accounts Receivable Associate position. Both in the classroom and on the job, I have shown that I possess these qualities. As an accounting concentrator at Northeastern University's College of Business Administration, I had a 3.0 GPA overall—but my GPA in accounting classes was a 3.6. Many of my classmates struggled mightily with Intermediate Accounting in particular, while I received an A- in this rigorous course. As far as being trustworthy, I would encourage you to contact any or all of previous employers, whose contact information is available on the enclosed reference page. I am confident that each supervisor will indicate that I was entrusted with depositing considerable amounts of cash after closing for the night and locking up the place of business. Additionally, I am proficient with Excel: I am extremely confident and comfortable when creating formulas, charts and graphs—even pivot tables.

Close the cover letter by reaffirming your interest and noting how you prefer to be contacted. This is fairly straightforward.

Example:
I would welcome the opportunity to interview for the position. To arrange an interview, please feel free to contact me via e-mail at *m.brooke@neu.edu* or by phone at 617-555-8800. I look forward to hearing from you soon.

Revise, edit, and proofread your cover letter and resume with extreme care—then find some other competent people to double-check your work. I can hardly overstate the importance of this point. When reading cover letters and resumes, managers assume that they are seeing the very best that you have to offer. Intentionally or unintentionally—fairly or unfairly—an employer will infer a great deal from your cover letter. The potential employer will develop perceptions regarding your communication skills, attention to detail, level of interest in the job, self-awareness, and selling skills based on the quality of your cover letter. Accordingly, your cover letter needs to be perfect grammatically and completely free of any typos. I knew of one employer who would simply circle typos with red pen and return the cover letters to applicants, noting that "you clearly lack the attention to detail that we seek in all potential recruits." Most employers won't be that harsh—they simply won't bring you in for an interview.

A COMPLETE EXAMPLE OF CREATING A COVER LETTER

Remember the resume of Meghan Brooke, from the sample resumes at the end of Chapter 2 of this book? Because we always must try to match a specific individual to a specific job description, let's use her resume in writing a sample cover letter. As for the job description, let's say Meghan is applying for the following job:

GLAMTONE PUBLISHING
Glamtone Publishing a leader in the publishing and distribution of medical textbooks and other health-related media products seeks a PC/LAN Support Associate to assist our 400+ end users with computer-related issues ranging from simple MS-Office issues to Intranet updates and ultimately more technical troubleshooting issues, including assistance with our Windows NT network.
Qualifications: All applicants must have familiarity with MS-Office, strong communication skills, and the ability to learn to use new technology quickly. Exposure to the following technologies is a plus but not required: HTML, Symantec Ghost, Windows NT Server, and TCP/IP. Looking for a team player with a great attitude who can handle a high-pressure environment!
Compensation: This position pays $32,000-$38,000 depending on pay and experience.
To submit a resume, please write to Louise Guardado at Glamtone Publishing, 145 West North Street, Southborough, MA 01234. No phone calls please.

It would appear that Meghan has some chance of getting this position: She believes she has all the required skills and at least one of the "plus" skills. She decides to write a cover letter.

The first step in writing this cover letter would be for Meghan to try to be honest with herself regarding her strengths and weaknesses for this position. Here is a quick checklist of some questions for a candidate to ask herself at this point:

1. *Why would this company hire me rather than someone else?* You want to focus on attributes that might make you stand out from other applicants if at all possible. Lots of MIS students have familiarity with MS-Office, for example, so that might not be the best primary selling point. For Meghan, her best bet might be to concentrate on her high GPA as a reflection of the "ability to learn quickly"—not everyone can say that they have a high GPA. Her customer service experience at two jobs—including the ability to learn quickly at Kohl's—would be worth citing as well.

2. *Why WOULDN'T this employer hire me, and can I do anything about that?* When looking at job descriptions, you can't just consider what jobs are attractive to you—you have to ask yourself how you can make yourself most attractive to the employer. You have to be honest with yourself—for example, could Meghan be beaten out by someone who has more of the preferred skills listed in this job description? Absolutely. Can she do anything about that? Maybe. If she really wants this job and has the time to do some additional research, she could take a few days to try to ramp up on the skills she lacks.

She certainly could learn enough about Symantec Ghost to be able to mention it briefly in the cover letter and discuss it intelligently in the interview. Reading a *Networking for Dummies* book or something shorter about Windows NT Server and TCP/IP obviously could make an impact. But isn't that a lot of extra work in light of the fact that she doesn't even have an interview yet? Of course it is. You have to be judicious about how much time you are willing and able to invest in each cover letter. However, if Meghan is completely sure that she wants a PC/LAN Support job, then doing some extra research on software applications is bound to pay off sooner or later. Doing research on the company also can help—though that would definitely be the kind of extra effort that is more of a one-shot deal.

3. *Is there anything I can reasonably do that will help get me inside information about the job?* If you were referred to the job by someone, you definitely should pump that person for information about the organization. If you're lucky, maybe they will even be able to tell you some useful facts about the organization's culture, the supervisor and/or interviewer, and the job itself. What do people really like and dislike about this job, this department, this organization? If you know some of these things, you may able to tailor your cover letter accordingly. At the very least, you could check out the company website or drop by the company and tell the receptionist that you intend to apply for a job—is there any general information available about the company. Taking any of these steps can reflect your willingness to go the extra mile as well as your sincere interest in the job.

Once you have made this kind of self-assessment and done what you can do regarding your "fatal flaws," you can write the cover letter itself. On the following page, you can see what Meghan's finished cover letter might look like:

March 24, 2003

Ms. Louise Guardado
Glamtone Publishing
145 West North Street
Southborough, MA 01234

Dear Ms. Guardado,

I am writing to express my interest in the PC/LAN Support Associate position, which your organization posted with the job listings made available on Northeastern University's HuskyCareerLink system.

As you can see on the enclosed resume, I have numerous skills and qualities that make me a great fit for this position. Despite challenging myself with a double concentration in MIS and Marketing, I have managed to maintain a 3.6 GPA at Northeastern University. I believe that my excellent academic record reflects my ability to learn quickly a critical soft skill for any new hire in a technology-oriented position. In my previous job experience, I have an outstanding record of providing patient and effective customer service. This experience should prove invaluable when providing PC support to Glamtone's end users.

While I have not had the opportunity to work with Symantec Ghost or with Local Area Networks, I have done extensive reading on these areas since reading your job description. As a result, I have a good but basic sense of how to re-image a computer as well as an understanding of networking fundamentals.

I would be delighted to come in for an interview at your earliest convenience. From my research on Glamtone Publishing, I know that you are a young, fast-growing publisher with a reputation for producing highly professional medical materials. After talking to Beth Shawerma in your Human Resources Department, I would say that I especially would enjoy working in the fast-paced environment at Glamtone.

Please feel free to contact me via e-mail me at *m.brooke@neu.edu* or by phone at 617-555-8800 to arrange an interview. For your convenience, I am also enclosing my references I urge you to contact them to verify anything on my resume or to ask any questions about my work and academic history. I look forward to hearing from you soon.

Sincerely,

Meghan Brooke

WRITING A COVER LETTER AS A CO-OP STUDENT

In some instances, students also may write cover letters when attempting to find a co-op job—most often with a co-op employer who is not currently involved with a co-op program. When writing this kind of cover letter, you will need to provide a brief explanation of what you are seeking as well as why hiring a co-op student would be a good move for the employer.

With this in mind, let's revise the previous letter. In this case, let's assume that Meghan is a co-op student seeking an MIS position for six months. We also will use this example to show how to write a more general cover letter. As noted earlier, you also want to write the cover letter with a specific job description in mind. If this is not possible, however, this might be a good approach.

Look at the following page to see this co-op job search cover letter in its entirety.

March 24, 2003

Human Resources Manager
Glamtone Publishing
145 West North Street
Southborough, MA 01234

To Whom It May Concern:

As a current student at Northeastern University, I am writing to express my interest in seeking a computer-related co-op position. In my academic program, I go to classes full-time for the first half of the calendar year. Then I am available to work full-time hours for over six full months, starting work this year on Monday, June 15 and continuing through December. I am willing to consider any position that involves computers—some examples would include PC/LAN support, database design/development maintenance, Web page design and maintenance, QA testing, or positions that use computers to help other functional areas such as marketing and finance.

From your perspective as an employer, there are many benefits to hiring a co-op student. In these economically uncertain times, co-op student workers represent a relatively short-term commitment. Co-ops are cost-effective and benefit-free human resources. Co-op students are trying to build great resumes and references for future employment, so they are highly motivated workers as well. Lastly, co-op hires are a good way to keep a recruiting pipeline active in anticipation of brighter economic times in the future.

As you can see on the enclosed resume, I have numerous skills and qualities that make me a great fit for a computer-related position. Despite challenging myself with a double concentration in MIS and Marketing, I have managed to maintain a 3.6 GPA at Northeastern University. I believe that my excellent academic record reflects my ability to learn quickly—a critical soft skill for any new hire in any technology-oriented position. In my previous job experience, I have an outstanding record of providing patient and effective customer service. This experience would prove invaluable if your Network Administrator needs assistance in providing PC support to Glamtone's end users.

I would be delighted to come in for an interview at your earliest convenience. From my research on Glamtone Publishing, I know that you are a young, fast-growing publisher with a reputation for producing highly professional medical materials. After talking to Beth Shawerma in your Human Resources Department, I would say that I especially would enjoy working in the fast-paced environment at Glamtone.

Please feel free to contact me via e-mail me at *m.brooke@neu.edu* or by phone at 617-555-8800 to arrange an interview. For your convenience, I am also enclosing my references—I urge you to contact them to verify anything on my resume or to ask any questions about my work and academic history. I look forward to hearing from you soon.

Sincerely,

Meghan Brooke

FINAL THOUGHTS ON WRITING A COVER LETTER

You may never have to write a cover letter during your co-op career, but sooner or later you will have to know how to write one effectively. Even when you learn about job opportunities through friends, family, fellow students, or former employers, you frequently will be asked to write a cover letter when submitting your resume.

Given that cover letters are time-consuming, there is nothing inherently wrong with having a few cover letters that you re-use to some degree—certain elements might remain the same across quite a few letters. However, don't EVER send out a cover letter without making sure that you have changed ANY customized references! Imagine how well it would go over if Meghan took her Glamtone cover letter and reworked it for another position—but then left the reference to Glamtone in the final paragraph!! All of a sudden, the first impression that the other employer has of Meghan is of someone who lacks attention to detail and who may indeed be flinging dozens of cover letters at jobs with only slight modifications.

Because organizations listing jobs may get tons of replies—especially in a tough economy—a little persistence can't hurt. If you hear nothing from an employer within a few weeks, you might try writing a brief, upbeat note to reaffirm your interest—particularly if you think the job is a great fit.

Several years ago, I replied to a *Boston Globe* ad listing a position that appeared to be an unusually good match for me at that time. Two weeks passed, and I heard nothing. I wrote a follow-up letter and politely acknowledged that I was sure that the company was very busy—particularly given that they were a small company listing a position emphasizing their need for a medical writer/project manager. I reaffirmed my interest in the position and briefly recapitulated why I was a great match. Then I just said the honest truth—I was only a few weeks away from needing to make a commitment regarding a teaching position that was available to me. If the position was filled or if they were uninterested, I understood completely. If not, I urged them to arrange an interview as soon as possible.

Within three days of mailing the letter, I received a call to arrange the interview. Three interviews later, I got the offer and accepted it. I often wondered if that would have happened if I had simply waited however long it might have taken for them to acknowledge my first attempt. After the second letter, they definitely knew that I was seriously interested. I don't know any organization that wants to hire someone who only wants the job a little!

APPENDIX C
Additional Resources

In this last section of the book, I have included a few different materials that I have found useful in teaching our Introduction to Co-op courses at Northeastern University as well as sheets that I have developed for working with my graduate assistants and students over the years.

Fine-Tuning Your Resume may be useful for students wishing to do a spot-check of their resume or for instructors who want to tip off students to common errors. I developed **Common Interview Problems and How To Solve Them** after I had conducted over 200 practice interviews. It's easy to tell if an interview is good, bad, or somewhere in between, but it can be difficult to articulate exactly *why* an interview is lacking. I have given this to my graduate assistants when training them, but it also can be helpful for co-op and career services professionals in their efforts to get beyond *symptoms* of interview difficulties to identify the root problems. The problems are listed in approximate order of frequency, and each is paired with plausible solutions to the problem. The **Interviewing Scenarios** and **On-The-Job Performance Scenarios** can be provocative for classroom discussion in small or large groups; I also use this as make-up assignments for students who miss classes. Lastly, **You Make The Call! Decide What To Do If YOU Were The Co-op Coordinator** is an exercise designed to make students walk in our shoes as career professionals. Understanding the roles of all constituencies—student, co-op/intern, co-worker, supervisor, internship/co-op coordinator, and career services professional—is critical to becoming successful as a developing student employee. This exercise may help students appreciate the delicate balance that co-op and career professionals must maintain when providing services to numerous students and employers.

FINE-TUNING YOUR RESUME

Is your resume REALLY all set? Here are a few elements to double-check—they represent solutions to the most common mistakes on business co-op resumes!

1. Make sure to include your month and year of graduation (i.e., May 2007).

2. Add *References Provided Upon Request* as last line.

3. If appropriate, consider adding *Financing ____% of Education Through Part-Time and Cooperative Education Employment* to bottom of education section.

4. Write out your degree: Say "Bachelor of Science Degree in Business Administration" NOT "Bachelor of Science Degree in Marketing" (or "Studying Psychology," etc.).

5. Have start and end dates for all jobs.

6. Add computer skills section if missing.

7. Add interests section if missing.

8. Differentiate between majors, concentrations, and minors if necessary.

9. Make sure jobs are in reverse chronological order (with some exceptions).

10. Add GPA if at least 3.0.

11. At most, list GPA to two decimal places (3.25); okay to round up or down (i.e., 3.072 can be written as 3.1).

12. Unless beginning sentence, write out numbers that are ten or smaller, write 11 or higher as a number (i.e., 15, not fifteen).

13. Use bold and italic fonts to improve aesthetic quality of resume and add variety. Consider using something other than Times New Roman to be different (i.e., Arial, Garamond, Century).

14. Make sure each sentence or bullet point has a verb—almost without exception.

15. Avoid obvious phrases such as "Responsibilities included."

16. In job descriptions, don't just list transferable skills: each sentence/bullet point should include an aspect of what you actually did.

17. Add quantitative and qualitative details to bring your job description to life.

18. Go beyond summarizing your duties: What were your *accomplishments* in the job?

19. Follow a format from this guidebook: NOT a MS-Word template or the advice of your brother's girlfriend's cousin's friend who is really good at resumes!

20. Be consistent in font, capitalization of words, and bolding; be consistent in the use of periods at the end of sentences.

21. Spellcheck **and** proofread!

COMMON INTERVIEW PROBLEMS and HOW TO SOLVE THEM

	PROBLEM	SOLUTION
1.	Being "interviewer dependent" (Quality of your interview depends on quality of interviewer)	• Answer general questions with specifics. • Use specific stories and examples. • Make interview a "conversation with a purpose."
2.	Lacking a strategy	• Write down three reasons why YOU should be hired for THIS specific job. • Discuss these reasons ASAP in interview (i.e., when answering open-ended questions).
3.	Inadequate research	• Prepare as if your life depended on it! • Weave your research into answers and end-of-interview questions.
4.	Answers aren't helpful	• Always tie answers to company's needs according to job description or coordinator.
5.	Negative nervous energy	• Preparation • Practice • Put Energy Into Presentation. • Maintain external focus.
6.	Weak opening and/or closing	• Don't rehash resume. • Articulate strategy early. • Prepare ten good questions. • Bridge to close of interview.
7.	Getting stuck; blanking out	• Ask clarifying question. • Don't be afraid to pause. • Use note page (carefully).
8.	Raising flags for interviewer (making statements that raise concerns about whether you are appropriate for the job)	• Preparation • Focus on positives, always. • If negatives must be discussed, choose ones that won't hurt you.
9.	Insensitivity to interviewer --Talking too fast --Lack of "active listening" --Digressing from the point	• Practice speaking style. • Pause, especially after key points. • Respond to verbal/non-verbal cues. • Stick to what he or she *needs to know*.

INTERVIEWING SCENARIOS

Scenario 1
An interviewer asks you what pay rate you'd be seeking for this job. What do you say?

Scenario 2
A person from a company calls you to invite you in for an interview. You set up an interview for 10:00 a.m. on Friday. "Oh, by the way," the interviewer says. "It's Casual Day here on Friday, so no need for you to get dressed up." How do you dress for the interview?

Scenario 3
You agree to have an interview at 11:45 a.m. on Tuesday. But then one of your professors announces that there will be a review session at the same time, and you know it will hurt you to miss it. What do you do?

Scenario 4
You need to come up with an answering machine message that will convey your professionalism to the prospective interviewer. What would it be?

Scenario 5
You arrive 15 minutes early for a 9:00 a.m. interview. You had to get up early to be there on time, so you are annoyed when the interviewer doesn't appear until 9:25. What do you say about the interviewer being late?

Scenario 6
You are an international student. At some point in the interview, you are asked: "Do you plan to stay in the US after graduation, or will you return home?" How do you respond?

Scenario 7
It is Monday, June 8, and you don't have a job lined up for summer/fall. You are hoping to get an offer from Cornell Products but know you probably won't hear until early in the next week. The phone rings, and you get an offer from Carew Software. It's not a bad job but definitely one that you would turn down if you had an offer from Cornell. What do you say to the person from Carew Software?

Scenario 8
You accept a job from Pandolfo Hospital in mid-May and feel pleased to line up your co-op job so early. Two weeks later, though, you get a surprise offer from The Drury Rehabilitation Center that had interviewed you in early May; you had given up on getting an offer from them, but now they are offering you more money and a better job than the one at Pandolfo. What do you do?

ON THE JOB PERFORMANCE: SCENARIOS

Scenario 1

Jeff is interviewed by a large company for a finance job. The job description is vague and mentions little more than the need for a 2.0 GPA and dependability. The interviewer asks only one or two questions; at the end of the interview, Jeff asks a question about the hours. Jeff is surprised to receive an offer two days later. He accepts. After two weeks on the job, he finds he is very bored. Assisting the finance department, he spends most of his time filing and faxing and photocopying. He does a little data entry each day, but this is not difficult to master. Though he has agreed to work for six months, he thinks he will go crazy doing this kind of work for that long. What should he do now? Should he have done anything differently?

Scenario 2

Lucinda is feeling a little annoyed about her job. It seems like her boss is picking on her about everything she does. First, her boss complained that Lucinda would just sit at her desk when she ran out of work, instead of asking for more. Then the boss gave Lucinda a hard time because Lucinda thought she should double-check on how to do a bookkeeping procedure that she was trained to do a week before. Today, she is especially irritated because her boss gave her a hard time about being late a couple times this week. Lucinda had come in only five or ten minutes late: Several full-time employees did that, but she didn't see the boss talking to them about it! At 11:00 a.m., Lucinda puts aside the spreadsheet work that she has been asked to get done as soon as possible, and she calls her co-op coordinator to complain. What would you say to her if you were her co-op coordinator? Do you think Lucinda is being treated unfairly?

Scenario 3

Ya-hui is asked to back up all of the voice mail systems on the tape. It is a long and tedious job, and it is not her favorite thing to do. Yet her job for the most part is good: she is learning a lot about networks, databases, and hardware. Her boss comes in as she is finishing up with the voice mail back-up process. "Do you like doing this sort of work, Ya-hui?" the supervisor asks. How should she reply?

Scenario 4

Steven is an Arts and Sciences student studying communications. He lands an internship with an advertising agency. He is excited about the job. During the interview, the manager told him that he would be working on an important event and get to use his writing skills on developing some promotional materials. Three weeks into the job, he finds that all he ever does is clerical work such as faxing or sorting through file cabinets to throw out dated material. He feels that the employer hasn't kept their promise, and he is tempted to simply up and quit. How should he handle this situation?

Scenario 5

Oliver, a sophomore, is hired to do a fairly low-level job at an animal hospital. He knows it is not the best job, but he wants to get a good evaluation. What are some suggestions that you would give him?

Scenario 6

Sarah is feeling uncomfortable about a situation at work. As one of three co-ops working in an accounting group during tax season, Sarah has enjoyed her job—especially the opportunity to work overtime hours for good pay. However, she finds it odd that she is usually the only co-op asked to work overtime. A few days ago, her manager praised Sarah's work and offered to give her a ride home because it was dark. This morning he suggested taking her out to dinner to thank her for putting in all the overtime hours without complaint. Nothing has "happened," but she feels uncomfortable about being asked out to dinner by her boss. What should see do? If you were her co-op coordinator, and Sarah told you about the situation, what would your response be?

Scenario 7

Upon being hired for a co-op job, Max is told by an HR person that his hours are 8:45-5:00 Monday-Friday, including 45 minutes for lunch. His pay will be $12/hour, which multiplies out to $450/week before taxes. Max hits it off with a couple of full-time co-workers during the first few weeks of the job. One Friday they tell Max that they're going way across town for a long lunch—does he want to come? It's obvious that they'll be gone for a couple of hours. "Don't worry about it," one of the co-workers says. "The boss won't be back today, and HR will never know." Max isn't sure. At times it does seem like he's the only one who's usually taking just 45 minutes for lunch, and he's definitely the only one carefully tabulating his hours to submit on Monday morning. What should he do?

Scenario 8

Here is what one student wrote after being fired from a co-op job a few years ago: "I am currently a fourth-year student at NU. I recently was let go from a co-op position that I held for more than a year. The reason for my dismissal was because I received an e-mail that was deemed unacceptable by my employer. I was let go on the same day that I received this e-mail and forwarded it to my NU account.

"The purpose of e-mail in a co-op environment is as a way to conduct corporate communication—not for the social benefit of the co-op student. This is the lesson that I hope you take from this case. Actually, I think I was lucky—the situation could have been more serious. When I opened the e-mail, someone could have seen the letter and been offended—maybe offended enough to charge me with sexual harassment. Or I could have forwarded the e-mail to a co-worker by accident.

"Here are my suggestions for future co-ops: Use e-mail only for work purposes, and if you must send e-mail to friends, then keep it simple. Ask them what time they want to meet after work, for example. Also, you may want to make sure that your friends do not have access to your e-mail address at work. Additionally, don't check your other e-mail accounts while at work if at all possible: You never know what someone might send to your personal e-mail account."

QUESTIONS FOR DISCUSSION:

1. Do you think the employer was ethically and/or legally right in choosing to terminate this student? More specifically, is it ethical and/or legal for an employer to read a co-op student's e-mail?
2. What would be some examples of an "inappropriate" e-mail?
3. Besides e-mail, list other examples of ways in which a student could be doing something "inappropriate" at work.

YOU MAKE THE CALL!
Decide What To Do If YOU Were The Co-op Coordinator

In the following scenarios, assume that you are the internship or co-op coordinator. As such, you are the go-between working with both students and employers, trying to do what is fair and right in all situations. You also are trying to ensure that your students are learning to become professionals, which includes being responsible for their actions. With all of this in mind, how would you handle the following scenarios?

Scenario 1

Alex is a student that you worked with in September. Co-op was scheduled to start on September 21, and he came to your office for the first time on September 17. When asked why he started so late, Alex said, "I was real busy, and then I had to drive to Florida." When you ask if he can get the guidebook today and bring in a resume tomorrow, he says, "I can buy the guidebook, but I have to go to Delaware tomorrow for the weekend. I can come in Tuesday."

When he comes in Tuesday with a resume—two hours late for his 9:00 a.m. appointment—you go over it and make many corrections. Alex says, "Since it's so late, can I call you at home tonight to go over the revisions?" You say no, and he accepts this.

You help him get a job at Premium Life Insurance in the suburbs. He is pleased because it is near his house. But less than two weeks later, he calls you in an irate mood because he has been fired. "They screwed me over!" he says repeatedly. "I was late ONCE because I had a flat tire... what am I supposed to do about that? And they said I used the Internet too much, and I only went on it TWICE, when there was NOTHING to do. My supervisor thought I was great...It was HER boss that fired me. I think they wanted to get rid of me because I'm a co-op; they want full-time people."

You call his immediate supervisor. She says that Alex was 1) on time twice during just eight days of employment—he was typically five to 15 minutes late; 2) using the Internet after being specifically warned not to do so until he had mastered all the basics of customer service, which he had not done; 3) accidentally hanging up on customers after keeping them on hold for a long time, then denying that he did it; and 4) coming in very tired, wearing wrinkled clothing, with his shirt tail hanging out, etc. She had tried to work with him but others had become fed up and demanded that he should be terminated. She found it hard to object.

The two versions of this story differ dramatically. Alex is coming to your office shortly. He has already said he wants to talk to another of your employers about a co-op job, as they had wanted to interview him but had been unable to because he accepted the job with Premium Life. How would you deal with Alex? What would you say to him? Would you send his resume out to another employer?

Scenario 2

Tarek is a student in looking for an internship starting in early January. It is early December, and you have not seen him for months. He comes into your office with a resume and says he wants to interview for a position at Gillette that just became available. You look at the resume for the first time. It has several typos, and the format doesn't match the guidebook, but these are mistakes that could be fixed fairly quickly. And you see that he actually has much more experience than the seven or eight students who have been looking for jobs since referrals began in mid-October. There's a good chance he would get the Gillette job. How would you handle the situation? Would you refer his resume to Gillette? Whether you would or would not, what would you say to this student?

Scenario 3

It is mid-November, and you are incredibly busy with employers on campus, students making decisions on offers, and other students who are at various stages of the process. The phone has been ringing like crazy, maybe 40 to 50 times today alone. On top of everything, there is a long line of students waiting to see you this afternoon during walk-in hours. You are trying to deal with each student efficiently, but you also need to keeping things moving along.

Around 4:00 p.m., a student from another coordinator named Samantha comes into your office. As she sits down, she says, "I've been sitting here waiting to see you for over an hour." You tell her that you're sorry for the inconvenience and point out that it is an extremely busy time of day and time of year.

Samantha says, "Well, you're never available. I've come in every afternoon this week, and you're either not in your office or there's a long line ahead of me. Everybody else is getting jobs, and you haven't even looked at my resume yet. This isn't fair."

Checking your files, you see that you have a record of Samantha contacting you just once this quarter. Three weeks ago, she left a message saying that she needed to see you as soon as possible. You left a voice mail for her saying a few days and times that you were available. There has been no contact since then.

You have some good employers coming in over the next week or so to interview students. It would be easy enough to put Samantha on a few interview schedules. What would you say or do?

Scenario 4

A new employer has interviewed four of your students for a new position with a small company. "I don't know who to hire," the employer says. "Why don't you tell me who the best one is? I'll just offer the job to whoever you think."

You consider the candidates: **Carol** was in your Introduction to Co-op class last year and came to all the classes but otherwise doesn't stand out in memory. **Henry** is a transfer student who has made a good impression on you so far in terms of his attitude and professionalism. **Mark** seems to have the most relevant job experience on his resume, but he strikes you as being kind of difficult: He made a stink over needing to revise his resume several times. **Sarah** did well in your class in terms of class participation and attendance, but you and she agreed that her practice interview was only about a "5" on a scale of 1 to 10. What would you say to the employer about whom to hire?

Scenario 5

You receive an evaluation for Nkeche Adebiyi, who recently completed a position with your second-largest employer. It's an extremely negative evaluation, giving her low rankings almost across the board. You ask Nkeche about it, and she says, "Oh, it's just because my immediate supervisor didn't like me for some reason. But her boss thought I was terrific, and we were great friends.

You call up her boss. The boss acknowledges that she thought Nkeche was okay for a while, but she now thinks that they just weren't aware of her shortcomings because the company admittedly did a poor job of giving her structured work in the first two months on the job. After that, though, the boss was amazed at how unproductive and seemingly uninterested Nkeche was in doing the work. She tells you that Nkeche has said to co-workers that she really doesn't like this type of work—she just does it because the pay is good. There also were issues with her using a company cell phone to make personal phone calls, apparently to her boyfriend.

Nkeche basically denies all of this when you confront her with these new facts. She says that this manager now has it in for her because she received such negative information from her immediate supervisor. You tell Nkeche that you're concerned about referring her out to another employer; she pleads with you to give her another chance. You're not sure: It's a bad economy, and you can't afford to alienate any more employers. What do you do?

Scenario 6

A company in Sarasota, Florida calls you up in December looking for a co-op student to work for six months in their Florida office. They offer competitive pay, free housing in a furnished condo with weekly maid service, a free rental car, and a chance to get lots of experience and training with Lotus Notes and MS-Access. They are willing to hire up to four students to start in January.
You only have about 12 students still available. And while your life will become much easier if they get jobs as soon as possible, there's no question that some are stronger than others. In fact, there are only three candidates whom you are fairly positive would do a very good job in this situation. And with a phone call you learn that one of them just accepted a job. The others started looking late and/or have come across as having attitude problems, difficult personalities, and a questionable work ethic.

If you send all 12 resumes, the chances are that three or four students will be hired, and that you will be very nervous about a couple of them. This will be the first time students work in this department: A highly successful performance by one co-op likely will increase the number of jobs available in the future. But if even one student goes down to Florida and trashes their rental car, performs poorly, or runs into significant problems either at work or in company housing, the company may never hire another student from your program. Still, you need to help all 12 students get jobs. What would you do?